Warm Cup

Inspirational Insights on Relationships and Life

of Wisdom

gathered by

Dori Jones Yang

Warm Cup of Wisdom, Inspirational Insights on Relationships and Life

Book cover design by Kathryn Campbell
Printed in the United States of America.

ISBN: 1495411451
ISBN-13: 978-1495411458
Library of Congress Control Number: 2014907954

Published by East West Insights
Kirkland, Washington
www.eastwestinsights.com

CONTENTS

INTRODUCTION

IMAGINE YOU'RE HAVING a lively lunch with nine of the wisest people you know. In some ways they are a lot like you, except about twenty years older. You can ask them all the questions you'd like, to help prepare yourself for what comes next in your life.

These are people you admire for their wisdom about everyday matters—getting along with others, bouncing back after tough times, dealing with awkward emotions, and navigating painful situations. Although each one is different, they personify the way you'd like to be in twenty years—remarkably resourceful and resilient. They make aging look so appealing!

At a time of life when you're dodging bumps in the road, juggling stressful situations, wrestling with big decisions—or just wondering where you'll find the strength to tie your shoes! —they reassure you that it's possible to come out the other side not only whole but well.

Wouldn't it be great to ask them how they did it? To get insights that would help you map out the road ahead? You could ask them to not only offer advice but also share stories of how they learned life lessons. If they struggled with mild depression or anxiety, how did they overcome it? When tragedy hit—the death of a loved one, a divorce, a sudden loss—how did they cope, and what did they learn over the years about better ways to react? How did they take a troubled relationship and turn it around? What little daily techniques do they use to control anger, stop judgmental thoughts, and return to a calm, kind mindset?

At midlife, in our forties and fifties, many of us don't have such sages to light the path for us. We've seen how-to books galore relating to the first half of life: finding passion, seeking a job, planning a wedding, launching a career, having a baby, starting a business, and raising children. But what about the second half of life? When we reach middle age, whom can we turn to for advice? We could all use a "Circle of Stones"—a set of elders who have navigated these waters before us, who could give us tips on how to get the most out of our mature years.

That's what I aim to provide with this book. I chose nine women—all of them fifteen to twenty years older than I am—and asked them these types of questions. I harvested their wisdom and collected it in this book, using their words. In every case, I emerged from our discussions with new insights that I hope will make me a wiser person.

I am fortunate to know many wise women. I met these nine through my church. In fact, my particular church has such a rich abundance of wise women that I had trouble choosing just nine for this book. I wish I could have interviewed more. They are all, like me, white, Christian, suburban mothers. Their beliefs and experiences shape how they live their lives, and their responses are steeped in the values of their faith. But this is not a book about religion or Christian teachings; in fact, several of these women dared to speak up to change attitudes within their church. Most of their insights reflect common values shared by men and women of many backgrounds: care of the self, care of others, and a desire to get along. The questions I asked were designed to bring out useful, thoughtful wisdom about how to understand your own needs and improve relations with the people in your life.

Your sages may look very different. If you open your eyes, I suspect, you may find wise people in your life, too—perhaps through your extended family, your community, your workplace, or some association or cause you've joined. If you do, I urge you to be bold and ask them similar questions.

But perhaps you don't see such people in your life. Many of us have mothers and aunts who can't or won't share their wisdom with us. Some have lost their mothers or have trouble communicating with them. It can be hard to truly hear your own mother's advice when she's been nagging you for years. Often, it seems, we spend more time with people our own age or our children and their friends. Few of us take the time to sit down and ask for insights from the older generation.

I believe it's important to validate and value the wisdom of our elders. Too often postretirement women (and men) are overlooked and belittled. American society lionizes youth and beauty. Wrinkles and gray hair are problems that need fixing. What's more, women of my generation (the baby boom and beyond), who grew up with feminism and workplace opportunities, sometimes disparage the generation ahead of us, figuring they never faced the issues of work/family balance or identity shifts the way we did. What I found, though, is that once we reach midlife the issues we face aren't that different; we have a lot to learn from mothers and aunts, over a warm cup of tea.

Much of the world's wisdom resides in older women. Yet older women are less likely than men to broadcast their wisdom through books or lectures. From my experience, most women's wisdom comes out in one-on-one sessions. On average, they outlive men, so by definition there must be more wise old women than wise old men. Why aren't we hearing more about the wisdom of older women? Perhaps we've shut our ears. Or perhaps we just haven't asked.

I wish I could introduce you in person to the nine women featured in this book. During our long, lovely lunch, with plenty of coffee, tea, or wine to sustain us, you would meet these wise women:

Patsy + **Isabelle**, an amateur actress who adopted two children, lived in Egypt several years and now appears in local television commercials.

[handwritten: Lyn] ✦ **Eva**, an activist who survived a painful divorce, lives her values by making friends with Muslims, theosophists, and *qigong* experts, and hands out flyers on a street corner every Saturday, making the case for peace.

[handwritten: Carol] ✦ **Ruth**, a poet whose husband suffered from a degenerative disease that warped his personality, emerged from that experience as a gentle soul who inspires her friends.

[handwritten: Barbara] ✦ **Susan**, a pragmatist and community leader, recently endured a mother's nightmare: a grown son who died of cancer just two months after diagnosis.

[handwritten: MaryAnn] ✦ **Katherine**, a consultant who married Mr. Right and raised two children, discovered at midlife that she had fallen in love with another woman.

[handwritten: MaryAnn] ✦ **Joy**, a feminist who learned to speak up for women at the national level when her church was going through wrenching changes, surprised herself when she felt gratitude after the pain of her husband's death.

[handwritten: Mary] ✦ **Anna**, a chaplain who recovered from childhood abuse, returned to school at midlife to work in a hospital helping others deal with pain and grief.

[handwritten: Joan] ✦ **Jane**, a Yale-educated biology teacher, morphed into a local and national church leader able to smooth over differences on the most controversial issues.

[handwritten: Penelope] ✦ **Pamela**, a preschool teacher, discovered leadership skills she didn't know she had and steered a school through eighteen years of growth, despite her recurring bouts of depression.

I have given them all pseudonyms to protect their privacy. It seemed the right thing to do, since they were remarkably honest and open with me.

Early on, one of the women asked me an important question: What do I mean by "wisdom"?

Do you know people who got older but not wiser? I sure do. In thinking about those people in my life—and what makes me think them unwise—I came up with my own definition of wisdom.

A wise person does the following:

+ Figures out a way to maintain positive healthy relationships with most friends and family

+ Understands and respects others' needs and feelings

+ Knows how to let go of and rise above bitterness and past troubles

+ Finds a way to express anger without letting it poison relationships

+ Knows how to emerge from negative thinking and overcome it

+ Takes charge of his or her life and finds purpose and direction

+ Helps others with a good heart and intention

+ Seeks a way to make the world a better place

+ Thinks and behaves toward others with humility, kindness, and compassion

These are tough things to do at all, let alone consistently and well. But I think it's worth trying.

Starting with this definition, I created a list of twenty questions. Some topics are positive, like wisdom and happiness, while others appear negative, like failure and regret. Other questions deal with life events: raising teenagers, dealing with adult children, or finding new direction at midlife. But in all cases, I asked these sages to talk about how they weathered the storms of their lives, and I found their answers both hopeful and inspiring.

I hope you do, too.

The Twenty Questions

1. How would you define wisdom—and why?

2. What do you recall about a time when you learned to speak up and make sure your voice was heard?

3 What are your basic beliefs about happiness? Has your thinking about that changed? Do you think happiness is due to circumstances, inborn traits, or choice?

4. During tough times, what sustains you and gives you energy and hope?

5. Can we truly forgive? If so, how?

6. What choices did you make at midlife to move in new directions? How do you make a meaningful life for yourself after retirement and/or empty nest?

7. What choices have you made about work (whether paid or volunteer), and how does that reflect your core values? What advice would you give others about finding their calling during early adulthood and midlife?

8. What did you learn about parenting when your kids were teenagers? What advice could you give to somebody else who's going through a rough time?

9. How do you manage your relationship with your grown children?

10. What are some keys to a good, lasting marriage?

11. When you're feeling estranged or angry with someone, what have you learned about healing relationships? What have you learned about dealing with people you perceive to be difficult?

12. Over the years, what have you learned about how to deal with or express your anger?

13. When you're feeling negative—whether depressed, anxious, judgmental, or self-pitying—how do you get yourself out of it?

14. How do you bounce back from setbacks or failures?

15. What have you learned, from your own experience and that of your friends, about the best frame of mind for facing aging and health declines?

16. How were you able to move on after a deep loss in your life and what have you learned about ways to cope with personal loss?

17. What do you wish you had done differently, particularly in your forties and fifties? What regrets do you have?

18. How has faith informed or guided important moments and decisions? How has your faith changed over the years?

19. What do you do to try to "make a difference"? Do you do volunteer work or give back to the community? If so, what is the importance of that to your life?

20. When are you most at peace? What keeps you moving forward into hope? Where do you look for inspiration?

Chapter 1

Seeking Wisdom

WISDOM HAS BEEN on my mind for the last several years. During my early fifties, after years of work and child rearing, I began reordering my priorities. Instead of chasing credentials or recognition, I've shifted my goals so that I try to embark on projects that make a difference in the lives of others. These days I focus on the deeper meaning of life and my lasting contribution.

My friends in their forties and fifties assure me that I'm not alone in this. Many of us, it seems, view the second half of life as a fresh opportunity to do something different. Often, one of our goals is to acquire wisdom.

I'm convinced that wisdom and knowledge are *not* the same thing.

We attain knowledge through classroom learning, studying, and training that fills our heads with what we need—or want—to know. By knowledge I mean facts and figures, plus the ability to analyze them and make judgments about them. It's the specialty of scientists and university professors. Knowledge is great. I'm a big proponent of lifelong learning.

But wisdom is different. Wisdom grows out of life experience, dealing with other people, and coping with our own emotions. Wisdom guides us toward meaning in our lives.

In our younger years, we were learning like crazy about how to get good grades, adapt to the workplace, and perhaps raise children. Every day, it seems we were busy figuring out how to tackle new problems and adjust to surprises. We were gathering experience but didn't have much time to ponder, to make sense of what was happening at lightning speed.

In the second half of life, the pace sometimes slows down, and we have the perspective of years. It's a good time to pursue wisdom.

Like knowledge, wisdom is not a set point. You don't get there and say, "Great! Did that. What's next?" Wisdom accumulates gradually and involves a deliberate response, an effort to learn and grow. Not everyone learns from mistakes. Some are ground down by the stress, while others find unexpected strength and learn to bounce back with resilience. I want to know: How do they do it?

I like to think I'm wiser today than I was ten or twenty years ago. Ideally, I'd like to be wiser ten years from now than I am today— and even wiser twenty years from now. That's why I embarked on the journey of this book.

Not everyone views wisdom the same way I do, so when I sat down with these nine women, I decided to start by asking each about wisdom. I was eager to hear what they had to say.

THE QUESTION

How would you define wisdom—and why?

Katherine

When I was in college, we had to define our philosophy of life. They asked us to define wisdom and virtue. I said, "Wisdom is knowing what your gifts are, finding out what you brought into the world that's uniquely yours. Virtue is using it to make the world a better place." For a college kid, that was pretty cheeky, wasn't it?

I might say the same thing today. One of the hardest pieces

about growing up—for me—was finding out who I am and not trying to be someone I am not. I have a friend who is a wonderful hostess, sets a gorgeous table, and cooks like a dream. I admired her tremendously and tried to be like her at different times in my life. But that's not who I am. To come to the place where you know who you are and what you have to offer, and then to be willing to offer it—I think I'd still go with that.

In the past, I put enormous, and unhelpful, pressure on myself to be like others. For whatever reason, I bought into that: how important it was to be this or that, according to what you thought the rules were—what you thought would make you popular, safe, or whatever.

A joy of being my age now is that I've arrived at a place in my life where I've come to terms with who I am. I don't say, "Screw it, world! Like me or leave me," because I do care, very much. Still, I have a stronger sense of who I am and less inclination to worry about the things that I might not be.

Jane

Wisdom is the ability to make careful decisions about any number of things but particularly as they affect people's lives—and to be able to discern the difference between truth and falsehood.

Earlier in my life, I would have equated wisdom with knowing a lot about many things. If I knew the botanical names of the plants and the butterflies and the quails, then I would have an aura of wisdom. But now I am aware of those who demonstrate wisdom in relating to people, in interacting with people—in all sorts of ways affirming and encouraging others.

To me, wisdom has become a way of making decisions and doing things that enhance our lives and the lives of people around us.

Anna

Wisdom is seeing. In most cases it comes from life experience, but there are some young people who are remarkably wise.

An example is my granddaughter, age twelve, who has a disability. When she was about seven or eight, she wanted to swing on the monkey bars. She tried and tried but couldn't quite do it. I was standing nearby, trying to help her swing her arms. She said, "Grandma, I need to talk to you." She took me to a bench on the playground and said, "Grandma, sometimes people just have to do things for themselves." How did she know that? It's wisdom. She's expressing what's real for her.

It's true that there are some older people who are not wise. But you know what? It's usually their emotions that are messing them up. That's the experience I've learned.

What makes most people wise is hardship—living through pain. If one chooses to grow with it, one learns. Wisdom is perspective, being able to see a bigger picture while in the midst of something.

Wisdom comes without one knowing that it's coming. If I make a remark that's wise, I don't always necessarily know that's what I'm doing. The wisest people don't know they're wise.

Yet we can learn to act more wisely. Here's something I learned: I call it the "potty training" set of processes. This is true for all of us in learning. Initially a person is "unconsciously incompetent," like a baby in diapers. And then as you learn, you become "consciously incompetent." In regard to toilet training, that's when the toddler tells you he's already gone. And then comes "conscious competence." You know what you're supposed to do, and you're trying very hard, not always getting it right. The final step is "unconscious competence." You say or do the right thing without even thinking about it.

This is a metaphor for any kind of learning that is not cognitive.

You can call it wisdom. But it's also learning from experience that you have to develop new habits.

Joy

When I was twelve, my father got a job in Asia, and we moved halfway around the world. This was scary at first, but quickly I fell in love with the sunny tropics and the gentle people who expressed gratitude to Americans for liberating them from wartime occupation. I also found my new friends in the American school in Manila to be super. I had the fortune to have a challenging education in those formative years.

Then in my junior year of high school, Dad informed us that he had completed his job and we were going to move back home to America. "Oh no!" I whined. "*This* is home. I want to stay *here* with my friends!" But he insisted. "We're going to complete our journey around the world, see more of Asia, Africa, Europe, and then we'll sail into New York Harbor on the Queen Elizabeth." I had to agree that that sounded pretty great.

I cried the day I left, but the very next day, new adventures opened up for me and my brothers. This is perhaps the first little bit of wisdom I was aware of, realizing that when a door shuts, there's no point in spending a lot of time lamenting the closed door; it's better to turn around to appreciate what's next. This is a marvelous gift that my parents gave me, early on—a sense of adventure about the promise and wonders of the unknown.

In December of 1950, I was sixteen, slim, enthusiastic, and sported a five-year tropical tan and pierced ears (horrors!) when I became the new girl at a suburban high school near Washington, D.C. After having been fully involved in the social life of my school in the Philippines, I had a wrenching experience of being excluded and ignored by the girls. The boys had no such problem. They called me "Manila Lil" and apparently found me exotic. This might have made the girls even more upset, I suppose! I struggled to make sense of this, and it taught me a huge lesson. Those popular girls felt threatened by me, and they didn't even try to get to know me. So I looked around at all the other students who were also rejected, people who were of another race, who dressed oddly, or looked or spoke a bit differently than they did. I ended up with a slew of oddball gal pals and got to know that people very different from me were often very interesting. I decided to never, ever reject someone's friendship without getting to know her first.

During this difficult year, I was fortunate to have family support and the maturity to realize there was nothing wrong with me. In Manila, we lived in a culture where new students showed up often: every week or two a few new families arrived, and a few left. That was the nature of living abroad. I learned that the status quo was not forever. I gradually learned to prefer change, rather than hanging on to the status quo.

One other thing that I learned was that it is important to spend quality time alone. That's a good way to figure out who you are as an individual. Constantly being with "the gang" may mean thinking, saying, and doing the same things as others.

It took me a long time to learn to value how important it is to ask questions. I didn't challenge the system very much at first probably because my older brother was good at that. He was rebellious, and he thought it was fun and hilarious to be so. My reaction was then to embrace the opposite, to be a "good girl."

Nevertheless, I craved independence. I loved to be alone—to climb up and sit in the apple tree, hike to the lake or cliff and sit there looking over the world, meditating, thinking, dreaming, and writing poems. I have many warm memories of alone time. And I still do all that, except for the tree climbing.

Only later, in my twenties, did I begin to ask challenging questions like "Why are women not appreciated?" I could not accurately visualize what was going on around me; I only knew that opportunity was there for men—for my brothers—but not for me. This led to many changes in my thinking and my life.

Susan

Part of wisdom is how much you are able to stand apart from what is going on and see the ultimate goal or the bedrock of a particular situation in which you find yourself. It's having a sense of perspective.

Wisdom shows up when you can draw back instead of impulsively rushing in. This could be a personal relationship, a meeting with a complex agenda, or a sensitive communication with someone. If you can draw back enough, you can see it as a whole instead of a part.

When I was younger, I tended to jump in quickly. I had more soapboxes that I could mount than anybody in the world. Now I know that I only have so much emotional energy, so I can only put time and effort into a limited number of things. When I was young, I had all the answers. Now that I am older, I have loads of questions.

As a young person, you feel like you can impact the whole world—and that your work is going to make profound changes. Fortunately, the young use their creativity and impulsiveness to create remarkable things and give us the strength to go on. That impulsiveness is wonderful, but it lacks perspective.

Part of growing older is being realistic. You realize that you can't change the whole world, but you can affect your own life. To me that's one of the biggest things. Look at alcoholics or at people who have compulsive behaviors. Those people can change only when they decide within themselves to make the decision to do something about their problem. The change must come from within.

You can rationalize all kinds of things. We have friends at this point in our life who are totally denying that they are ever going to die or ever going to get sick. Well, we are not going to get out of here alive. There is no way. It scares me to see some folks that we know—and I love them all dearly—saying, "Well, I'm fine today, and I've got a good health record and I'll be fine." No you won't. Maybe you will live to be ninety-two, but you're not going to be able to do what you did when you were twenty-two, forty-two, or sixty-two. That's just the nature of the human body. Denial is another wonderful way of rationalizing whatever we want to rationalize.

We just don't know how long we'll live, how long we'll be healthy. We can't. We can't deny our mortality. Nor can we deny our fallibility. We are not infallible—or immortal.

Ruth

Wisdom, to me, is learning from the people surrounding you. Although I still rant and rave over injustice, I am learning that life is cyclical. My version of wisdom includes the constant reassurance that God's kingdom will come.

Pamela

Growing up, I discovered that I really like to learn new things, but I can only learn them in teeny tiny increments. Over the years, those little increments have grown on each other, and pretty soon I realized that I know more than I thought I did, which feels good.

I think that wisdom is life experience. Living in the moment helps to soak in what you're doing and have it be part of you— rather than just skirting over the top of everything.

It's also problem solving. For instance, a really big one for me came when our children grew up and went on with their lives. The holidays, especially Christmas, were always a big deal in our family. I always said, "You all come" to the grandmas, uncles, all the kids, and their friends. Well, then the kids got married, and they had their own plans, which changed everything that I've treasured. It took me several years to figure out that I can't change this. *This is the new thing in our family*, I told myself. *I'm going to have to think of it in a way that can nurture me, and yet let go of those traditions.*

Our son and one of our daughters got married the same year. Our daughter's new family always celebrated on Christmas Eve, *always*. Well, that wasn't going to change. And our son's new family always celebrated on Christmas Day.

So here I was just feeling lost, wondering how do I live with this? After a couple years of steaming, I suggested that we have our family Christmas gathering on an entirely different day. Each year, we celebrate on a different date because Christmas moves around and their work schedules move around. So now we choose a date; we don't exchange gifts, but it is our day. Our family's gift to each other is being together.

I guess you could say that wisdom is realizing what it is you really want and finding a way to get it even if it requires some compromise.

Isabelle

I've often thought of wisdom as intelligence. Somebody who was really intelligent was wise. Intelligence has always been important to me. I thought I didn't have it and I wanted it. To be really intelligent was to read *Paradise Lost* and understand it.

Wisdom, I think, is something that accumulates, that you learn by being with people, by living. You get wiser because you've had all these experiences. I think any kind of experience adds to what you learn. Whether it's bad, whether it's good, they all add to who you are.

I thought of that recently when I was with a group of women at my college reunion. They all had such different lives. I could learn from where their lives had taken them and how mine was different from theirs. They had turned wise in different ways. These women were all from small towns and they still are. Some of them live in the same houses they bought when they first married. But they had all travelled.

Wisdom must have to do with meeting people from other places and other cultures. If you get out of your sphere of what's right for you, you find out that what's right for other people is not the same.

I was lucky because I got to live in a totally different culture when I went to Egypt. My husband, Sam, had a job there, and we had to move our family over. Because of that experience, I grew up. I really grew up.

When we got to Egypt, it was July, and it was hot, really hot. I was spooked and the kids were spooked—except my son. He went out and had a great time. My life was turned upside down. Nothing was the same. Life became wonderful, but it took a lot of time. At first, the telephone didn't work, the electricity didn't always work, nor did the water. I guess I was growing in self-confidence and in my ability to deal with the unexpected. There were people in the house all the time because you were expected to have help. All of that made me wiser about people, and it made me grow. I wonder if you relate "wise" with "growing."

Slowly we met people and saw how they lived. We had a good friend who lived across the street who was an Egyptian doctor—a strange kind of doctor because the patients didn't pay very much money. The man who delivered our groceries on his bicycle was Coptic Christian, so he would find us pork and other things not easy to find in a Muslim country. He took us to his home once to meet his wife. You meet these different strata of people. There's really poor and really rich in Egypt, not much in between. So I was learning, meeting these people and finding out everyone's not like us in the United States.

Living overseas broadens your mind and helps you understand other people. But some of my college friends, who spent their whole lives in small towns, became wise, too. Maybe it's your outlook on life: whether you accept what's happening around you or you get uptight and start saying, "Oh, they're different. I can't deal with them."

My friend Ruth is a wise woman; she's been through so much. She's a wonderful listener. Being a good listener is being wise. Have you ever sat down with somebody who really listens? I'm not really good at it. But I try.

Eva

Could wisdom be a combination of intellect and intuition—with a determination to seek the greatest good? And wouldn't wisdom have, at its heart, love?

If there is any wisdom within me, I believe it originated with God, but very often it works its way to me by way of someone else. I think I can learn something from everyone—certainly the young. As a mother of two sons and a grandmother of four truly grand grandsons, I know for sure that wisdom isn't granted only to the aged.

At a particularly low point in my life, when someone close to me was busy pursuing happiness and in so doing disappointed me terribly, I found myself disgruntled with Thomas Jefferson's notion that we all have the right to life, liberty, and the pursuit of happiness. I thought, *Why didn't he say, "life, liberty, and the pursuit of intelligence"?* Then I thought, *I know some intelligent people who are not doing very well with that intelligence.* I finally settled on this: I wish Jefferson had written, "life, liberty and the pursuit of wisdom."

Some people are undeniably intelligent and have high IQs but don't seem to be very wise. Perhaps they have a low level of emotional quotient (what some have termed EQ). Perhaps they have trouble relating with or appreciating others. So wisdom must be about both intelligence and emotions—a head and a heart thing.

MY TAKEAWAYS

The diversity of these responses surprised me. Because these nine women come from the same community, they might appear similar to an outsider. But they certainly don't think in the same way!

Isabelle still equates wisdom with intelligence, while Eva learned the hard way that a super smart person can be very unwise in how he treats other people. Both Eva and Anna have noticed remarkable wisdom in children and developmentally disabled people, which seems to contradict my assumption that wisdom grows from life experience.

Yet there were clearly some common themes. Here are some of the gems I gathered from them about the meaning of wisdom.

+ Understand and value your unique self and what you have to offer; then be willing to offer it.

+ Take a moment to view things from a larger perspective.

+ Be realistic about what you can actually change, which includes your own attitude.

+ Realize what it is you really want and find a way to get it, even if that means compromise.

+ Step out of your comfort zone and learn from people who are different from you.

+ Realize that what's right for other people may not be the same as what's right for you.

In my experience, wise people tend to be humble—especially wise women. They don't shout from the rooftops or give lectures on wisdom. They just hold your hand and offer loving advice when you're going through a tough time. None of these nine women came to me and said, "Interview me! I'm wise!" Part of wisdom is understanding that we don't have all the answers.

I'm glad several of these women mentioned that wisdom involves asking questions and being a good listener. On this journey of discovery, maybe I'm on the right track.

Chapter 2

Speaking Up

WHEN I WAS in my early twenties, I was shy. As a beginner journalist, I had to get up my courage each time I picked up the phone to call someone for reporting. *Why should this important person bother talking to me?* I often wondered. An older editor set me straight. "They're not talking to you; they're talking to *Business Week*." That helped, but still I found it hard. Over the years, as I developed my skills as a reporter, my confidence grew. It took even longer before I was willing to speak up and assert my opinion.

Many women—more so than men, I've found—have trouble learning to speak up. Confidence and bravado don't seem to come with the female package. I suspect that was even truer for the generation of women who came of age in the 1950s and 1960s, when women's roles in the world were limited. Women also face social pressures to please others and therefore to keep our thoughts to ourselves.

Yet all of my chosen wise women had learned to speak up and be heard. I was curious to hear their stories of how they did this.

THE QUESTION

What do you recall about a time when you learned to speak up and make sure your voice was heard?

Joy

I learned about speaking up first from other women. I was the only girl in my family, and I did not learn this at home. I had played the submissive little sister. But by observing people I deeply admired in the community, I began to trust my own voice, my own self.

Girls are natural organizers of human relationships. We are the ones who plan the parties in grade school, and by high school, girls often control social life. In marriages it is often the wife who selects the dinner guests, and thus the circle of friends. But in large groups in the church, community, or at work, I saw that it was the male voice that seemed to prevail. When I taught, I noticed that girls were more often the quiet students, boys often speaking out freely, sometimes rambunctiously.

In the 1950s, most of my contemporaries got married right after college and set up house-keeping, some after a few years of work as a teacher, nurse, or secretary. I followed the same pattern, and I didn't think to question it until later. Then, when I was teaching high school English and journalism, I was dismissed for becoming pregnant. The principal told me, "We can't see pregnant women standing in front of high school students."

I began to recognize that doors opened for guys—not for gals. I noticed that those of us who were great leaders in college were not sought after to be leaders in the community or in workplaces. I graduated in 1956 and had not yet heard (in my quiet Midwestern college) of Betty Friedan. But I did notice the differences in job opportunity, and that it didn't seem to bother other women I knew. Seven years later, her book about the inequality of women in America, *The Feminine Mystique*, burst on the scene, but by then I was the very busy mother of three young children. Still, I read the book, watched, and listened.

When my children were young, I joined the American Association of University Women (AAUW) to be more involved with strong women who addressed issues in the world. I also became active in Girl Scouts to help shape a stronger program for my own daughters. I learned from women leaders in both of these groups. Not so in the church, not at first.

For many years, I wrestled with the issue of speaking up, particularly in the church. I was elected to serve on session (the managing board) as one of the earlier women elders in my church. The first time I became emboldened to speak up to the dominant (male) face of the church was at a session meeting in the early 1970s. The pastor mentioned that a member had given the church an American flag and brought forth a proposal to put it in our sanctuary. There was little discussion among the mostly male pastors and elders, except about how nice it was that someone would donate a flag. I didn't think the idea was so great, but I realized that no one else was going to challenge it.

So I took a deep breath and spoke up. I told about how my husband, Jeff, and I had just returned from China, where he spoke at a medical meeting. This was in the 1970s, shortly after the Communist government began allowing in a few Americans. One Sunday in Beijing, we searched for a Christian church to attend. Delighted to see us, the people ushered us to seats, handed us a Bible in English, and pointed to the scripture that was the subject of the day. As those Chinese Christians preached, prayed, sang—even though we could not fully understand—we began to feel like we were worshipping among our "sisters and brothers" in Christ. It was a warm experience.

At the session meeting I said, "You know, if there had been a Chinese flag in that worship service, it would not have been the same. Jeff and I were in the house of God, and it seems to me that national flags do not belong there."

The session voted to accept the gift of the flag but to place it in the fellowship hall, not in the sanctuary.

I was emboldened to speak because of my women friends, although they were not with me that evening. Behind the scenes, we had been talking about the importance of women speaking up. So afterwards I went back to those friends and they cheered for me.

Later, the national church of my denomination created a committee to address the need to hear the voices of women, and I was elected to the first Advocacy Committee for Women's Concerns. It was a radical move for a church, since our group of twelve was given the charge to address the General Council and the General Assembly on matters of concern to women.

I was a shy starter in this process at first, but I did learn to speak up and address the larger church, which had been oblivious to many issues of concern to women.

Eva

Gosh, I think that my husband leaving me for another woman prompted me to speak up. And I'm still speaking up about that! I'm much more outspoken now that I'm single again.

There were times, when I was married, that I would express a thought among the family that I married into, and very often the response would be one of two things: "Well, we've always known that!" or "That's ridiculous!" I often felt in that particular family, when I was younger, that I didn't have much to contribute.

These days, now that I'm single, I feel freer to say what I think.

Given a chance, I like to speak out about the Defense of Marriage Act. My defense of marriage doesn't involve denying loving, same-gendered couples a chance to share in the joys and challenges of married life. I have trouble with the idea of no-fault divorce. I think married folks should be people of integrity who honor their vows and each other.

Another thing that has me speaking up is our nation's proclivity to wage war. Our involvement in ill-conceived, poorly executed wars disturbs me deeply. I can't keep silent about that. If I could sing, I'd join the Raging Grannies, but the best I can do is speak out.

I'm also apt to raise my voice when people who profess to be Christian preach right-to-life yet say nothing about innocent life being taken in preemptive war, drone strikes and such. I can't abide that.

Isabelle

I've had to speak up more since my husband, Sam, died. Now that I think about it, I did him a disservice when he was alive because I always wanted him to make the decisions, even about which restaurant we would go to.

That comes from my upbringing. My mom was French, and there were four of us daughters. My father was definitely the dominant person, with a very bad temper. My mother would say to us girls, "Yes, we want to do that, but we will wait for the right time to ask him." It was always, "ask him," of course, not "decide." I think that I felt a carryover from that attitude.

In my day, it was a totally different world. The man was very much the decision maker in my family and I think in most families. They controlled the money. My mom didn't even know how to drive. Growing up with that, you think, *Oh, it's the guys who decide.*

Coming into my voice was a gradual thing—after I started doing theater. I did the high school senior play and then two plays in college. After graduation, I taught school for a while. Then I stopped working when we adopted my daughter Sandra. After that, I didn't do any acting until I was forty-seven, when we moved to Egypt. They had a little expatriates' theater. Sam and I both got involved, and it was fun. I thought, *I really want to do this.*

I was a pretty good mother and wife, but I always felt I was a bad teacher. Becoming an actress was really freeing. So from then on, that's what I did. I've always felt that if I had learned more at the beginning, if I had been trained in acting, it would've been heaven.

When you start acting, you think, *Oh heck, this is easy. You just learn the lines.* I was in Egypt, and we were all amateurs. But it took me so long to figure out how to hone my acting skills. Still, it was a wonderful feeling, belonging to a group doing something we all wanted to be good. I always have loved that about the theater: it's people coming together, working really hard, relating to each other as different characters and putting on a great performance together.

Speaking out in those roles also helped in other parts of my life.

I've always felt reticent. I always felt that people knew more than I did. As a child, I was a mediocre student, and I've always felt not quite smart enough. I never had a lot of confidence in myself until I started theater.

Pamela

When I was young, I wanted to be part of that big crowd, the popular kids, and I just wasn't. I had a hard time with conversation and speaking up. *Never* did I like to answer questions in the classroom. I wasn't very self-confident about knowing the answers. I didn't want to make a mistake. Plus, the thing to do was *not* to raise your hand and draw attention to yourself.

I went through college that way, too. I didn't do much speaking up in class. I had a few friends that I could talk to and did, but I didn't feel like I could stand and speak in front of a group. I didn't ever want to do that.

After I got married, I realized that my husband was a workaholic, so taking care of our three children was pretty much left up to me. That's when I became more outgoing. It started to feel good. During those years, we had our kids in preschool at a co-op through the local community college. When you do that, you pay less tuition, and you also have to work in the classroom. In addition to that, I had a teaching degree, so I would teach a little bit—lead some songs and just play with the kids.

I found out that a co-op is an organization that needs a leader. We usually had a chairperson, a secretary, and a treasurer. Seeing as how I wasn't very good at writing—at least I perceived I wasn't at the time—I didn't want to be the secretary. And numbers were never my thing, so I didn't want to be the treasurer. So I volunteered to be the chairperson! I figured I had a little talent there. I was in my early thirties when I had that "aha" moment.

About that time, the pastor of our church had a little study, and we read the book *Please Understand Me*. In it was a test to figure out where you stood in life. My husband, Gene, and I took the test. The results categorized people as introverts or extroverts. At the time, I assumed that Gene was outgoing. He taught school, was active in the church, and went to meetings. In college he was in the drama. So I was surprised when the test revealed he was an introvert!

I found out that introverts get their energy in a different way. Gene got his energy from building things out of wood in the garage: he needed quiet time away just to regroup.

My test results declared me an extrovert, and by then I was feeling like *Okay, that fits!* I realized that I was an extrovert in my younger years, too, but I'd held back because I lacked self-confidence. As I grew older and became more able to have opinions of my own, say them out loud, and be in charge of a family, I learned to speak up.

As you go along and learn things in teeny tiny increments, pretty soon you know more than you did, so it gives you more confidence.

Jane

I come from a tradition where people, particularly women, speak their mind—not just speak but see the possibility of doing things. My grandmother was a suffragette who marched for the women's vote. My mother took things in her own hands that needed to be done for the family and for my father's business. So I really haven't experienced a sense of not having spoken up.

My mother's mantra was "You can do anything you set your mind to." When she was in college, she drank from a well of wisdom that said, "Every day, in every way, I am getting better and better." That was very helpful to her. But I think she struggled with not being adequate. I know she didn't have a lot of affirmation from my dad.

As for me, I am who I am and if you don't like it—tough. At least, I wish that were true. If I look back on my life span, I think maybe my identity was so important that it sometimes interfered with my ability to understand and empathize with other people—maybe even my children. I think I've gotten beyond that. I'm certainly more sure that it's all right to be who I am—that I am one of God's beloved, and therefore I can extend that to other people. That's something I've learned in life.

I relate it to becoming older. It is a growing sense of confidence that you are okay, and you don't have to keep struggling to prove yourself.

Many times in my life, I've jumped into a new task that I was not prepared for. I always have the feeling that I'm faking it. For example, I'm playacting that I can run a meeting. I really don't have the foundation for this. I'm a fraud! There is a sense in which I do this, even today. What I realize is that this willingness to step in can also serve God's purposes. That my stepping in also brings other people to step in, too. It's not like somebody's going to find out I'm a fake.

I have taken on some things that I haven't done very well—things relating to the church, parenting, or work. I realize that I wasn't the greatest teacher in the world in all cases. Today, I'm more accepting of that. I'm able to say, "It's all right." At the time, I sometimes pushed it away without dealing with it. That sense of being a fraud was underneath there.

My self-confidence has increased with age and heightened my awareness that I don't have to work at it so hard, that I can be supportive of other people and see the possibilities of good outcomes in different ways of doing things.

Anna

I was used to saying what I thought other folks wanted to hear. So learning to speak for myself was a new one. It didn't happen until I went to seminary. Each class was like a seminar—we would read a chapter and the next day everybody was expected to contribute. So I had to learn to express myself. At first, I had a hard time. I was in my fifties before I did, and now, watch out!

I grew up in the era when women were number two in the household. They went where men went and did what was best for men.

Everything revolved around that idea that "He is the important one and we are here to serve." That's the way I was raised and what my husband's expectations were. It was a major growing period—going through therapy and seminary at the same time. Talk about remodeling!

Therapy had already started that process; I was shocked when I began to recall serious abuse from my childhood. In therapy, I realized there were two parts of me: what I was and what I was needing to be. It was a caterpillar-to-butterfly moment, a lovely period of time, very eye-opening, very affirming. It was interesting to find out who I was.

Healing is always surprising, for all of us. It's a lifelong process.

As part of clinical pastoral education (CPE), you learn about yourself. Also, you learn to hold your own in a group because they have undirected, interactive group time every week. No rules. Pretty soon everybody gets free with their words. It helps develop your ego strength. You learn to rely on your own sense of yourself and what you believe. I learned to say, "This is what I know. This is what I think."

At the same time, you had to be open to constructive criticism about what you could do better—because you could always do it better. It's like a hand of bridge; there's never a completely good way to play it. There is always room for improvement. We didn't have to be perfect. We were just learning.

I learned a lot through CPE, therapy, and seminary. That's how I became much more me than I had ever been.

Ruth

In my family, I was known as the shy little sister. I am fortunate to have been in a loving family, two marriages, and a church community where I felt that I could speak up about those things that were important to me.

It isn't easy for me to speak before a large audience, but as an adult I think I've often been vocal about my feelings, including my political feelings, one-on-one.

For instance, I was just speaking to my next-door neighbor, a lovely young woman who is Dutch. She and her husband just returned from Holland, where they spend their summers. We were talking about the state of our country and how awkward she felt to be over there, seen as representing the United States, including the bad aspects of which she despairs. My neighbors are not connected to a church, nor are they religious. However, that morning, I did seize the moment to say, "Heidi, one thing I struggle with is that, as a committed Christian, I resent the fact that there is a whole other representation of Christianity. The exclusivity and judgment that conservative Christians show is so foreign to what I believe Jesus Christ intended." I wanted her to know. She said, "I've often wondered about that."

Yes, I have learned to speak up, but what's changing for me is that I'm more able now to calm down about some issues and let some of it go.

Susan

When my husband was doing his medical training in California, we joined a church, maybe three-quarters of a mile away from the duplex where we lived with our two little boys. I belonged to a women's circle and was doing Bible study, and we enjoyed being there. The minister of that church ended up being less than ethical. He betrayed confidences from the pulpit. A couple of women that I knew quite well were just shattered from the things he said and did. The whole congregation was in a terrible uproar. This was in the spring of 1963.

The presbytery held a meeting to discuss the difficulties that had arisen. Some of the women wouldn't speak up and explain what the minister had done. They said to me, "You have to speak for us." So I did—even though I was hugely pregnant at the time. The vote was very close, in favor of letting him stay. Still, the presbytery decided that the church was too divided; the minister had to resign.

For me, speaking up has never been a problem. Part of it was because my parents believed in me and they respected my opinions. As a consequence, I have always felt like I had an opinion that was of value.

That's not true of some other women of my age. I was different because my parents and my husband nurtured me. Many women are hampered by parents, siblings, or spouses who don't believe in them, tend to put them down, or cause them to lack confidence. I don't know why some lack confidence. Part of it may be related to physical body type. This may sound really crazy, but I've noticed that people who are tall tend to be more confident. And I have always been tall.

We are all individuals. The general run of women in my generation was perhaps more quiescent, there's no question, and we came of age in an era that was rife with paternalistic attitudes and institutions. But that didn't mean all women were that way.

Katherine

What caused me to speak out? Being the good church woman who discovers herself in a relationship with a woman at a time when the church doesn't think that's so cool. In fact, some of the people who thought I was cool wouldn't think so if they knew this.

I had to stand up, speak out, and tell my story in an effort to say to the church: "While you're having this intellectual conversation about who is okay and who is not okay—to be ordained in this case—I need to tell you that you are talking about me. I will tell you how that's affected me and other people like me." It's one of the saddest chapters in recent church history. I've met people whose lives are still wounded because the church community that they grew up in no longer has room for them, and they haven't found one that does. It's a very sad thing, and it was worth it to me to expose myself.

It was hard speaking at the session meeting at our church. I had recently started attending and didn't know everybody. Homosexuality was the hottest issue of the day. I knew that my pastor was sympathetic and that some of the members would support me, but there were many I didn't know at all, and I wasn't sure how they might judge me.

After that, when my pastor said, "Will you come and be one of the speakers at the next presbytery meeting?" I almost died. It was like I was going to stand up there and take off every stitch I had on. This was the issue being debated: Should openly gay people be allowed to serve as pastors in the Presbyterian Church? I was to speak in favor.

I had been involved with the presbytery for twenty years by that time, but for a lot of people, my experience would be totally new news. I had served on a number of committees, and I was chair of the commission that closed one neighborhood church because its membership had dwindled. So I had contributed a lot. I figured this was a time I could use whatever credibility I had to influence opinions of those who knew me and my commitment to the church. That was a time when I did.

Speaking at the presbytery was terribly scary. When I got there, they had a little meeting for the eight of us who were going to be the speakers, and I realized I was going to be the last to speak on this side. The person who was going to be last for the other side was a big, powerful guy, the head pastor of a very conservative church. Very intimidating.

I had my little two minutes to speak like everybody else did, and then they voted— against my position. I went home with my tail between my legs. I'm still glad I did it.

MY TAKEAWAYS

This question really opened the floodgates! In many cases, the story of how we first spoke up is one that defines us. That is certainly true for Joy, Isabelle, Pamela, Anna, and Katherine.

My stereotype about older women was both reinforced and blown apart. Yes, women of this generation grew up with different expectations before the spread of feminist ideas. I came of age just as feminism was washing over the country in the early 1970s, and I did not expect to defer to my future husband in every decision.

Yet Susan and Jane did not fear speaking up. They seemed naturally confident. Other women turned to Susan and begged her to speak for them. In both cases, they had supportive parents who valued their opinions or modeled the behavior.

Here are some pearls I gathered:

+ Learning to speak your mind can start with advocating for others, including your own children, as Pamela did.

+ Learning to express your views takes practice; sometimes you can learn this in class or at work, as Anna did. Ego strength is something you can choose to develop.

+ Being heard raises your confidence. When others change their behavior because of what you said, it starts to feel good and you are more willing to open your mouth.

+ Confidence comes not just from being affirmed but from struggling until you learn to do something well, as Isabelle did with acting. When you're good at something, you have the confidence to speak up.

+ If others put you down or don't believe in you, it reinforces your unwillingness to speak out. (Yet Eva somehow learned to speak her mind anyway!)

+ Having the support of other like-minded women can give you strength.

+ When you're shaking with fear and feeling exposed and vulnerable, it may be even more important to make sure others hear your voice.

+ Even if you think you're a fraud, step in anyway. The more confident and competent you become over the years, the more you're willing to step back and let others try things their way.

Chapter 3

Pursuing Happiness

WHO DOESN'T LIKE to talk about happiness? It's the end goal, isn't it?

Actually, I have an ulterior motive in asking a question about happiness. I've had spirited disagreements with friends over the nature of happiness. I like to think it's a choice: we can choose to be happy or we can choose to be miserable. One friend insists it's circumstantial: if you've had terrible things happen in your life, of course you are miserable. For example, it seems cruel to expect someone whose husband has died to perk up. Another friend assures me that it's a matter of genetics: some people wake up every morning feeling subpar, and it's a struggle for them to get to a mood that's neutral, let alone happy.

I listened to a Great Courses lecture series called "Understanding the Mysteries of Human Behavior," and the lecturer, Professor Mark Leary of Duke University, cited research that said our general state of happiness is about 50 percent genetic, 10 percent circumstantial, and 40 percent choice. How anyone gets such precise statistics is beyond me. Even when people win the lottery, they are ecstatic on the first day, but within a short time, they revert to their usual frame of mind. People who are naturally downbeat can't seem to stay happy, even when things go well. And people who generally see the glass as half full don't stay in sorrow as long, even after a tragic death.

Given the wide range of personalities among these nine women, I wanted to hear their philosophy about happiness.

THE QUESTION

What are your basic beliefs about happiness? Has your thinking about that changed? Do you think happiness is due to circumstances, inborn traits, or choice?

Eva

Some months after my "dispute" with Thomas Jefferson about pursuing happiness, to my delight I came across Jefferson's definition of happiness: "Happiness is not being pained in body or troubled in mind." Goodness, surely everyone should have the right to strive for that!

But, to me, there is more to happiness than a pain-free body and an untroubled mind. I think there is an element of joy in true happiness. And an element of gratitude. Having a sense of God in my life and in life in general—a belief in a greater good—increases my "happiness quotient." It helps get me out of despair. Any time spent with happy, healthy grandchildren, that's true happiness! I guess happiness may come about as a combination of circumstance, character, and choice.

Joy

As a child I was drawn to the word "happiness." Maybe because I was raised in the 1950s, when many movies had happy endings in which the young girl got married and lived happily like in fairy tales. There were no big expectations beyond that for any girl. They met, they married, the end. Now that is really depressing, but it was common in my era. If you reached twenty-one and weren't married or engaged, well, that was weird. I followed the cultural norm: married at twenty-one. Both our daughters did not marry until they were twenty-eight and had several jobs and several degrees under their belts, and they did not embark on their "progeny projects" until their mid-thirties. I am sure that it made them feel more fulfilled than I felt at that age, and probably happier. I did not start on my own "upgrade" until midlife, after our children were out of the house. Being happy certainly correlates with life satisfaction, I think. It took me a while longer, but I eventually got there.

In my later years, after my husband, Jeff, died, many people said, "It's too bad he died so young." He was seventy-four, which is not really young, although it is young if you are in as good shape as he appeared to be. He was a fit, healthy, and active man with the bad-luck ticket of cancer. He was a nonsmoker who got lung cancer. Not fair. So began my grieving.

Shortly after that I came across a quiz about health on the Internet, which claimed it would predict how long you will live. *Really?* I thought. I put in figures for Jeff's weight, blood pressure, exercise habits, and the food he ate to see if he should have lived longer. According to this test, he should have lived to age seventy-six. That is pretty close to seventy-four. The quiz asked if anyone in the family died of cancer and how close those relatives were. I began to recognize how much cancer was in his bloodline. He may have had all these great habits but had the bad luck to have the wrong genetics. That understanding satisfied me, sadly.

After that, I chose to take the test for myself. One of the first questions asked if I "chose happiness." I immediately answered yes and then stopped and thought, *Wait! How can I say that? My husband just died!* Then I thought, *No, this is correct. I am a glass-half-full person. I'm basically a happy person, but one whose husband has died.* It was an insight into knowing that although I was in a stormy period, yes, I could still say I was basically a happy person.

So even though I've had times when I felt unhappy, as most people do now and then, in general I do choose happiness. But is it a choice for everyone? I don't know.

Now fear, that's a biggie that affects happiness. At one point in my life, I chose to confront the fears I had felt as a child. I did not want them controlling my life. I am much more at peace and happier since I resolved those fear issues. Much later, after my husband died, quite a few people—mostly women—asked me if I were not afraid to travel alone or to stay at our summer house alone. That surprised me, that grownups would allow fear to take away their serenity in life. That is a choice, I believe, that you can make.

This is why I think happiness is a choice.

Isabelle

I had a very volatile family, and I always felt I had to keep things even. I was the one who would try to keep everybody happy. I've always been a happy person—or at least I always wanted other people to be happy. I try to make light of things and find a way to cheer people up some way. I do that with my children, too. They would say, "Mom, you won't talk about anything real. You try to slide over it."

I feel like I'm a really happy person. My younger sister seems like a happy person, and she's really fun to be with. So I don't know if it's genetic.

Some people open the door and take their misery right out there with them. I talked about that with my friend who visited me recently. Our husbands died within months of each other. But she's very isolated, and she's still miserable. She said, "You're always such a happy person." And I said, "I just choose to be that way. I say to myself, 'Are you going to choose to be sad or are you going to choose to be happy?'" That's just what I feel.

Some people evidently can't choose, or why would they not try to see the brighter side? Why be miserable when you can try to find something else? Sometimes it just means finding a distraction from all the pain.

Pamela

I've struggled a bit with happiness because I also have depression, and when I'm depressed, it's really hard to be happy. But my basic well-person is happy. I see things in a positive way. Some people have the "happy gene." Sometimes it feels like I have it, but not all the time. I have some friends who just simply are happy all the time. I am still trying to achieve that goal.

You know, to be happy, you don't have to be "ha, ha, ha!" all the time. What I've learned through my depression is that happiness comes from inside. External things do not make us happy.

Being content with oneself is where happiness is. It takes a while to learn that.

You learn it one day at a time. Sometimes it's hard. When I'm depressed, I have really learned how to nurture myself, and that helps me with my happiness. Nurturing myself is learning to know that I'm the only one I can change. So if there's something that's irritating, I have to take the responsibility to figure out how to live with it rather than try to fix it.

You can't fix somebody else. That's a big burden lifted. Our kids helped me with that one! They taught me well.

Long-term happiness for me is to feel content with myself. I'm struggling with that once again because I'm going through another age change. All of one's life, you gain, you grow, you get more, and there comes a time when your body doesn't work quite right, and you get more aches and pains and you can't do as much as you used to. So life is diminishing in that way. But I'm trying to learn from Joan Chittister's book *The Gift of Years*: You need to be secure in yourself. You need to look at things from the inside. When you're content, things don't look so bleak.

Ruth

I think happiness is genetic—I really do. I see that in my present husband. He is able to think forward to the best and to see the best. Although he rants about politics, too! But yes, I think it can be genetic.

I have a modicum of that in me, I think, from my mother. For me, as I get older, a lot of happiness is coming to me from the fact that I really feel I can choose now how I spend the limited time I have left. A lot of that time is spent either being alone or being with people who are dear to me, and it is making a difference in my life. More and more, I realize that being in large groups is not appealing to me. It depletes my energy. It's a lovely, lovely time of life for me. I'm fortunate that my children are well and happy, and that makes a difference too.

Some people say happiness is a choice. But who's lucky enough to have the right genes? Off the bat, I think of a friend of mine who suffers from depression. Depression just stifles you. That is not a choice. I feel very lucky. By nature, in terms of contentment, I am on the average-to-high end of the scale.

Susan

I definitely feel that happiness is a choice. It certainly is impacted by things that are happening around you. But I have a friend who says, "Life is choices. Make good ones." The choices you make also impact whether you are happy or unhappy. And when you get to that place where you are unhappy, you have to look at yourself. Look back and say *What have I done? Where have I been?*

It all comes back to self and self-esteem. If you have made the choice to marry somebody who ends up abusing you, part of it is the choice that you've made; but the other part of it is the choice you make in continuing to allow it.

Happiness also depends on what you choose that satisfies you. Is it things, people, relationships, beauty? What gives you joy?

Katherine

I think happiness is a moment-to-moment thing. The word that comes to me now is more "contentment." I can be really, really happy in a moment because, boy, everything is just going my way, everything is in place. Like next weekend, when we will go down to a beach in Oregon with the whole family—there's a lot of happiness connected with that. I'm so glad that my children and grandchildren have accepted Marie and adapted to our situation.

Because I have suffered from depression, I don't think that happiness is a big goal. In my life, I've reached a state of deep contentment. I'm not giddy with happiness.

When I wake up in the morning, I think, *Oh, good! I get to have coffee*. I make a cappuccino, and I come out on the back patio with binoculars and my coffee. I say my prayers, and I watch the birds. I feel contented.

Happiness is when you win the gold medal; you're on the winners' stand and you're happy as punch, and you know that tomorrow you don't have to go for a gold medal so you're probably going to rest. Does that happy-as-punch feeling last forever and ever? No.

It's not like life is up on the mountaintops all the time. It's contentment that helps you through. Contentment has something to do with coming to terms with the terms of your life: who you are, where you are.

I'm very healthy—that's another thing. Frankly, I have been flabbergasted watching one of my dear friends go through breast cancer, mastectomy, and the treatments. She's acted as if she had a black eye and the bruise is gone and she's just fine. If I had a life-threatening illness, if I even had a funny little diagnosis, I would be very anxious. At this point in life, almost every day it's possible to hear about someone who has gotten the diagnosis or has died.

Contentment, for me, has something to do with having a lovely relationship—having someone around to share the minutia of life as well as the great stuff, and somebody who's around for the not-so-great stuff. That helps a lot.

Jane

There was a time in my life when I would have sneered at considering happiness something worth striving for. As an adolescent and in my early twenties, especially, I didn't believe in easy solutions for problems. I thought I knew too much to be just thoughtlessly happy about things. I was looking for a more sophisticated attitude or goal—something deeper and more philosophically rooted. I have always gravitated more toward thoughtful discourse than cheerfulness.

But happiness is more than just being cheerful. Happiness can be a deep condition, a well of security and a sense of comfort and confidence—to be able to look outside and say, "Yes, there's a lot of work I need to do out there in the garden, but aren't these gifts of beauty and plant growth wonderful?"

I am probably happier now. I see that being happy is a part of God's intention for our life. That doesn't mean that it will all just be clear sailing, but it's important to appreciate the wonderful gifts we have been given.

I have struggled with depression in my life. So I take a small dose of an antidepressant. It's actually an herbal supplement. My taking this is a way of saying I want to be happy, and I should work on that intentionally.

What I see—and this must have to do with my attitude—is that happiness is a God-given gift. We should not only take that gift and acknowledge it, but we should also pass it on to others or incorporate it into our living and our speaking in such a way that happiness touches other people, too.

Anna

Contentment is the word I would use, rather than happiness, and it requires focus.

I'm a person who is always looking at what's tomorrow, what's next. I need to work on being present. It wouldn't hurt if I were forced into some Zen or yoga practices to learn to center and be in the moment. I have never been very good at it, and I've been hoping to get better at it because I think that's part of contentment.

Contentment doesn't mean everything's "right" or that all my wishes have been fulfilled. We need to have dreams and wishes and move toward them if possible. But I am working toward contentment with what is, thanksgiving for what is.

Happiness—I associate that with moments of glee. Once in a while with music and worship, I get that feeling of "Oh wow!" and I float. That could even be a form of ecstasy. Music will do it for me, and beauty, the beauty of the earth.

There are those of us that are always pushing for something more, but I think everyone can learn contentment. I don't think genetics keeps us from being all we can be. Sometimes it equips us and sometimes it inhibits us, but it isn't a reason for not being all we can be. That's growth: learning what contentment is.

Contentment has to do with a choosing. Contentment is a conscious reality, an individual's choice.

We need to learn that it's not our job to keep other people happy; we need to see to our own happiness. This requires a sense of self. That is to say, a sense of one's own worth and what I've learned to call ego strength. One can look at one's self in the mirror and say, *You're okay. I like you the way you are. Yeah, you've got things to be changed. We'll work on those.*

Most all of us have some adjustment to do as an adult, to fill in the parenting that didn't happen. I think everybody ought to have therapy in the late teens or early twenties. It would be really healthy for people to develop responsibility for themselves, to realize, *It's my job now to see to my own happiness. It isn't somebody else's job.*

MY TAKEAWAYS

Happiness turned out to be controversial, and no two people saw it the same way. Four of the nine women see themselves as optimists, and the other five have occasionally struggled with depression. It's easy for glass-half-full people—like me—to say happiness is a choice. But clearly, depression is not a choice, as Ruth says. So whether it's because of nature or nurture, happiness does come easier to some people. Clearly, a happy frame of mind is some combination of inborn traits, circumstances, and—yes—deliberate choice.

I was surprised to hear that some think of happiness as fleeting, a giddy moment of glee that might seem a trivial goal, not worth pursuing. And although I love the word "joy," I can see that it, too, is a moment-to-moment feeling, not lasting.

The word "contentment" describes better the feeling I meant when I asked the question. Perhaps there's more an element of choice in being content with oneself.

Here are some insights to savor:

+ Satisfaction and contentment in life may be better goals than happily ever after.

+ When you are pained in body or troubled in mind, contentment is elusive. When you're in despair and can't climb out, you lose your sense of joy. Those are not always choices.

+ Still, it is possible to choose not to live in fear.

+ Contentment comes from inside; external things don't make you happy.

+ We can't make other people happy. If someone chooses to stay in misery or fear, we can't pull him or her out of it.

My favorite takeaway is Jane's statement: "Happiness is a God-given gift. We should not only take that gift and acknowledge it, but we should also pass it on to others so that our happiness touches other people, too."

Chapter 4

Sustaining through Tough Times

THIS QUESTION GETS to the heart of what I want to discover: What sustains people through hard times and gives them the resilience to carry on?

I know some people—perhaps you do, too—who can't seem to shake off the sadness, bitterness, or anger caused by some life-changing event. I have an aunt who was sickly as a child, lost her first husband in a car wreck, and lost her second husband to cancer. As she aged, she got more bitter and acerbic; once she screamed ugly words at my mother across a large, formal restaurant, all the while chasing after Mom with her walker. If she became a wiser, deeper person after reflecting on her suffering, that was never apparent to me. No matter how many years go by, some people can't let go. Yet others seem to bounce back—or at least crawl back.

What makes some people resilient? I'm sure it varies. The best way to get at this is to hear wise people tell stories of their own tough times and learn what got them through.

THE QUESTION

During tough times, what sustains you and gives you energy and hope?

Ruth

What sustains me? My garden, writing, reading, friends. I have a wonderful group of women friends. And of course, my family, my faith, and my church community.

All of these have been there for me through difficult times, including when my first husband's behavior became increasingly erratic, and none of us, including Tom himself, knew that he was presenting with a debilitating genetic disease. We stayed together for five more years, and then we divorced. Years later he was finally diagnosed with Huntington's disease. During all that time, I made decisions that were painful for him but necessary for his condition and, I admit, my well-being. I discovered a core of strength that I had not known was there.

It's partly the way we as women are raised, to value taking care of other people and not ourselves—especially in my generation. At some point, though, you just have to take a stand. It's terribly important to take care of yourself.

During his last years, I was able to be there for him when it was hard for almost everyone else. When he became unable to walk, we found a wonderful nursing home in Seattle, and that is where he died. He was courageous and kind until the end, and he lived many years longer than expected.

Of course, everyone does, sooner or later, go through hard times. Throughout my life, my faith in God has played, in a deeply organic way, a major role. I felt God's presence with me, with Tom, and with our children always. Our faith communities acted out that presence in so many ways. Our pastor at the time spent many hours with Tom—counseling him and being his friend. And a parish associate at the church where I worked did the same for me. For those who don't have a church community, it is important to build some kind of intentional community. I could not have done it all without those supportive people.

Small things, and an appreciation for them, brought hope to me: a latte on the way to work, the smell of fresh-ironed cotton, a narcissus on my desk—even paying the oil bill!

Joy

I do not know how a person without faith gets through the really hard times. When Jeff died, I discovered what sustained me. It took a while for me to see, but it was my faith in a living God, in Christ. That may sound hokey to you, but it became very, very clear to me.

It was through my friends who came to Jeff's side near the end, and to my side, who called, wrote notes, hugged, brought flowers from their gardens or food—maybe an entire meal or just a mocha or dessert. They were unrelenting in being there with us through the whole process. Some flew across the country to be here. Others stopped by for a few minutes, called, sent cards, or e-mailed. One young man, whom I'd known as a teenager, brought flowers to the door. Their love was palpable, powerful, and healing. These friends and loved ones embodied the living, loving presence of God, for me.

While Jeff was ill, I had to continue taking my dog, Pablo, on several walks a day. I remember walking in the rain one day in the beginning of my struggle with accepting what was happening and begging God to take me instead of Jeff. And that day I sensed Christ walking with me, alongside. He had always been there. I just didn't notice.

I often turn to reading poetry in hard times. Emily Dickinson is a poet I love, and one of her poems is about hope, which she compares to a feather. It is a lovely poem, but hope is not faith, hope is not solid. Faith is like a rock. For me, it *is* the rock.

Indeed, it was writing that also helped me. When my husband got the diagnosis of lung cancer, I knew that it would get hard. I instinctively knew how to use writing to help me through. I began writing when I was in emotional pain, while he was moving through his illness. I did not want to cry in front of him. The only way I could sleep at night was to first go in my office and write.

I often sat in front of the computer screen and let my fingers go. This is called unconscious writing, where you put your fingers on the keyboard and just let the words flow. You let go of your "inner editor," that critical self that says, "No, no, that is the wrong word. Stop! Can't you think of a better word?" Just get rid of that critical voice in your head and let out the pain.

When I do unconscious writing, I go into a space that is spiritual, religious, whatever you want to call it—maybe even magical. Whether it is my voice or God's, it not only gave me energy but released the pain. Sometimes I felt tears running down my face. The gift was that words came from deep inside and expressed my true feelings. And it was healing.

The next day, I would find poetry on my computer screen. Honest, unedited, raw, beautiful. Here were words that I could rearrange and edit later. They often surprised me with their insight. Sometimes what came out was the love, because there was lots of love in there.

The next unexpected experience of grief for me was "the tsunami." I am not at all sure if this is a universal experience. But after Jeff's death, when alone at home, I would let go completely, yielding to the grief, and I found it would hit me with a force of nature. Coming suddenly, the grief literally knocked me over, leaving me without any residue of familiar landscape, and washed me away. I let go, and I let it go. Only then could I get up and face the day. These tsunamis helped me realize—at the deepest emotional level—that life as I knew it was gone, destroyed. I would have to remake a new life.

After the tsunamis ebbed, I was left with a theological conundrum: Why did I feel *so deeply grateful,* when I was *so full of grief?* Oddly, I felt overwhelmed with gratitude. I asked many people, and finally one day I met the man who told me why. He said, "Look at what the Bible says in the Beatitudes: 'Blessed are those who mourn, for *they shall be comforted.*'"

Yes! What do you think when you see a new widow? That she is blessed? Yet that is what friends, family, and neighbors did for me. I was overwhelmed. Healing. Health. Wholeness. Life-giving love. I had to experience this to "get it." It was there, all the time.

Gratitude. I hope I can live the rest of my life in gratitude, grateful for each person in my life, each day, each moment of the day. As I was driving out to the lake today, I was thinking about this. If we are open to the present, we open up to the blessings that are right in front of us. So profound, so energizing, so simple. It makes every day a beautiful gift.

Each year I choose a word that will guide me through the year. I have used the word "gratitude" for four years, since it was so satisfying for me while I was moving through the most difficult time of my life. Each year I tried to find another word, but this one stayed and continued to be profound for me.

This year I found a new word. So I do know that I have moved on and perhaps even "remade" my world! Thanks be for tsunamis of grief, for tears, for loving family and friends, and for God's abiding love and infinite wisdom.

Katherine

Friends—I couldn't have gotten through my life without them, particularly my women friends. When my daughter had her second baby, I traveled to her city to help. The baby had been born, and they had just come home from the hospital. The same day, the phone rang and it was my son, telling me his wife had been diagnosed with cancer. I had this instant feeling: *I've got to let my chosen sisters know.*

There are eight of us who call ourselves "chosen sisters." Some I've known for almost forty years. We have seen each other through everything—alcoholic husbands, divorce, depression, illness, coming out, kids that disappoint, and kids that are wonderful. We've prayed together, laughed incredibly, and travelled together. That's what gets me through—as much so as my relationship with God.

I would say that my women friends are priceless. All of us have said, "Isn't it too bad that our husbands don't have the same sort of thing?" But men just do it differently.

And God. Clearly God. I just fall on my knees when I'm in a tough time. Theoretically, I don't believe in intercessory prayer *per se* because I don't think that God makes bad things happen to people. I had to think about this when our baby died. I can't see God up there saying, "Now for this newly married couple, I will give them this difficulty, a dead baby." I don't think God is in the details. But when things are rough, I'm right on my knees praying for the specifics—"Help me, help me, help me"—as much as the next person. I've never been disappointed, and not because I've had the answer. But I've had whatever it took to take the next step and walk through that tough time.

Eva

The courage I see in other people often gives me strength and hope. So many people I love and admire have gone through terrible things with amazing grace, patience, and fortitude. I find much encouragement in their examples.

Years ago I was training sales people at the Boston department store, Jordan Marsh. One of the messages we impressed upon trainees was "Enthusiasm is contagious." If you are enthusiastic about your merchandise, the customer will also be enthused. Later I learned that the word "enthusiasm" comes from the Greek word *entheos*, which means "God with us." Knowing God is with us is certainly encouraging. I expect that courage is contagious, too. I think I "catch" it from courageous people I am blessed to know.

I've often been afraid to do things that most people are eager to do. For example, I was afraid to learn to drive and didn't do so until I was about twenty-two, when my job required it. I figured *All those other people drive; I should be able to do it.* Also, I wasn't really sure that I was up to having a baby. I loved babies, but maybe it was enough to love other peoples' babies. Again, I reasoned, *All those other people have had babies; I should be able to do it.* I thank God that I did!

The Bible is full of stories about people who suffered, struggled, and managed to endure. Those stories give me hope. Having reason to believe that there is more to life than just this life also sustains me. I am very sure that there is life after this life, life after death. And it does get better. It *is* getting better!

Anna

What gets me through tough times is a connection to God and to people I respect, who respect me. I'm learning how important other women are; I didn't know that earlier in my life. Sometimes I need someone to talk to, like a therapist or pastor, someone to unload on. While I was a chaplain, it was a prerequisite that you have somebody to talk to. No one requires it, but any chaplain would be foolish not to have a therapist, a counselor, or a spiritual guide to lighten the burden and deal with any questions about successes and failures.

In those days, I relied mainly on my therapist. And sometimes I met with a group. Now it's a group, just three of us women chaplains. We get together as often as we can. We've been together so long that our lives are connected. We talk about work but also about our own personal struggles. As chaplains, we have a similar outlook on life.

Isabelle

When I'm dealing with something sad, I cry with the door closed. I'm not very good at expressing what I feel in front of people.

Sam was sick for a long time, and I was struggling. I could hardly move him. He was going to have to be put in a nursing home if I couldn't lift him anymore. I thought, *I can't put him in a nursing home! That would be the worst thing for him.*

Death was almost a relief for him. He fell down and then he died that day. That was in January. Just before that, we had spent Christmas at my daughter's house. Afterwards, my daughter told me my grandson broke down and said, "I don't want Grandpa to die." I thought, *He won't die.* Sam had fallen quite a few times before, and I'd call the fire department and they'd help me. The last time he fell, his heart had almost given out by then anyway.

When you live with someone for so long, you're just connected, even if you don't talk a lot. I never lived alone before, because I went from my parents to college to living with friends, then Sam. In some ways it was very freeing, and in some ways it was horrid not to have him here. I thought, *I have to figure out how I'm going to make it with just me.*

First of all, I had to figure out all the finances—I had been writing the checks, but he did all the rest. I had to figure out how to change the names on everything when he died. If I went somewhere, I had to make the reservations. It was overwhelming. Then when you get through that, you think, *Hey, I did that! I didn't think I could do that and I did.* It's freeing when you finally figure out you can do it, finding out you can take care of yourself.

A lot of what sustained me was that I connected with people in our church. I was always reticent to go because they know what they are talking about, and I didn't think I did. Isn't that strange? So I started going to a women's circle and Bible classes. I thought, *I have to be with people.* Then, I joined a drumming circle, which was wonderful. Then I connected with a group of widows and did things with them. They picked me up. People would invite me out. I think the church and my family have been wonderful. My two daughters live near me and the grandchildren and the great-grandchildren, too.

I have trouble with the praying and all that. I guess I never got it. I always believed that God was all around you. I knew that God was love, and that had to be all it was, my faith. Our pastor was great. He was going through all that awfulness at the same time because his wife died right after Sam. He called and talked. His idea of faith has helped me a lot because I always thought that I had to believe this and this and this, and that I'm not a true Christian because I don't believe everything I'm supposed to. He's been great because he's so open and accepting.

Birding has been wonderful for me, too. Sam had been gone for several months when I decided to go on a birding trip by myself. I'd never gone birding on my own. I found the shuttle and figured out how to get to the gathering point for a five-day trip. I took my wedding ring off because I didn't want anybody asking me about my husband. I was all by myself with all these people I didn't know, and it was wonderful. That was a turning point.

Birding was such a part of our lives. When Sam and I lived in Los Angeles, we'd go up into the hills every weekend. After we retired, all the trips we took were with a birding guide. So going somewhere to bird without him was hard. Still, after I was able to go on that birding trip by myself, I felt that I could do things and go places without him, and I would be okay.

Susan

During hard times, you put one foot in front of the other. You look at the hand that you've been dealt, you figure out all the possibilities, and then you work from there. But you don't avoid it. Don't think it's going to change overnight, because it's not.

I consciously try very hard to look at what's good and try to minimize the bad. I mean, I can criticize just like anybody else— I'm very happy to do that! But then I say, "Okay, this part of this is good, and this part of this is bad," and then I try to go from there.

When our son Peter died, yes, it was sad, and it's not what we had hoped for. But there were blessings around that, and God was with us. We had incredible support from the church, from friends, and from each other. My husband, Dave, and I went through it together, and we have chosen to look at all the blessings that came from that. So I do not mourn Peter's death anymore. Yes, I wouldn't have wished it, but I could tell you many things about that experience that I feel are incredible blessings.

Dave and I have always been a team because we have never had any family nearby; we've never been able to depend on anybody else but the two of us. Dave handled the medical part of it and saw that Peter got to his appointments. I managed to keep his physical being comfortable—feeding him and getting things clean. It took the two of us to make it work, but we worked together.

Our son was diagnosed the 7th of December and he died the 8th of February. The week after the diagnosis, he moved in with us, and he was with us until nearly the end, when he went into hospice for three days. So he lived with us for two months. I am so thankful we were still in our house; if we had been living here in the retirement community, it would have been a nightmare. Where would we have put him?

Of course, it was a nightmare. It was just a big blur. We just worked as hard as we could to make sure that everything went as well as possible. Because of what was happening in Peter's head with the cancer, he couldn't figure out his medicine, so Dave put up a chart on the bathroom mirror telling him what medicines to take when.

Peter was in terrible pain. The fact that he could be with us was a blessing. The fact that his brother was able to fly in to see him twice before Peter died—that was a blessing, too.

Being in hospice those last few days was a blessing. They were able to keep him comfortable. The night before we took him to hospice, I spent all night sitting up with him giving him medication to keep him at least halfway comfortable. Thank goodness for hospice, thank goodness for his doctor, who was wonderful. And the fact that he didn't have to spend another six months as a vegetable—that to us was a great blessing.

The people he worked with stood by him and brought him stuff. They appreciated him. His last three years of work were good years, very affirming. Before that, he'd had a very spotty work record, in and out of jobs that were unfulfilling. These folks thought he was just wonderful and told us how much they missed him.

And then came the crowning thing, which I don't talk about very often. I have worried about Peter since he was a little boy for one reason or another. After he died, I was sitting in church worrying about him, just because that's the way I am. All of a sudden, it was as if somebody poured warm water over me. There was a voice inside my head that said, "Peter is fine. He's with me."

So the blessings are overwhelming.

What sustained me? The fact that my husband was there. The fact that I knew that we were being supported by our faith. You know, God doesn't say it's going to be a rose garden; he just says, "I'll be there." And he was there and gave us the energy we needed. It was incredible the amount of energy we expended—just to keep things going, to keep food on the table that Peter liked.

Like many young people, Peter didn't attend church. He had faith of some kind, but I wasn't about to probe into it. We decided we would do his memorial service at his workplace and invite his coworkers. He worked for an organization that gives homeless and other disadvantaged people opportunities to train for jobs. At any given time, Peter was training six to eight people, making a difference in their lives. Isn't that what Christ asked us to do? Peter wasn't going to church, but he was living a life that made a difference. Not many people can say that; I certainly can't.

When he was working there, he would call me sometimes when he was upset about something. One time I said, "You know, you're the only adult that these people have really ever known."

"Well, yeah, but they're so hard to deal with."

I said, "When you were little, the three of you would take turns being bad, and I used to say, 'The one who was being the worst was the one who needed love the most.'"

He said, "You're right."

Later, his coworkers told us, "I can't believe how patient Peter was with these people." Yet that was not his nature.

Maybe he was ranting and raving, but he was giving of himself in a way that a lot of people don't. He was a very conflicted person, yet he was doing something that was valuable to many other people.

The blessings certainly outweigh the sadness.

MY TAKEAWAYS

I love the variety of these stories, and the way these women are willing to be vulnerable and open up about their most painful memories. How do you keep on living after an unwanted divorce or the death of your beloved spouse? How do you get the courage to take in a troubled adult son who is face-to-face with death?

I can't say I would ever have the strength or courage these women showed. But what I gained from talking with them is a toolbox of practical ideas.

+ Writing. This one appeals to me, as a writer myself. I love the idea that I could get through tough times by spewing out unconscious writing at my keyboard for fifteen minutes each night.

+ Friends. So many of the women mentioned their close women friends! Don't you love the notion of chosen sisters? If you have no sisters, or live far away from your sisters, you can choose close friends and be a sister to them.

+ Faith community or other intentional community. A sympathetic pastor, a women's circle, a group of widows— sometimes you have to reach out to find these folks.

+ Gratitude. This was a new concept to me, as it was to Joy. We can consciously be grateful for the small things in life, as well as the friends who bring flowers to our door.

+ Blessings. Who would think to count your blessings when your son is dying? I was amazed by Susan's story.

+ Faith. "God doesn't say it's going to be a rose garden. He just says, 'I'll be there.'"

+ Small victories. The sense of achievement when you figure out how to do something you never had to do by yourself before.

+ Exercise. Taking frequent walks or practicing yoga.

+ An appreciation of small things. Gardening. Reading poetry. Birding.

+ The courageous example of others. If they got through hard times, perhaps you can find the courage to plow through, too. Courage can be contagious.

These suggestions are concrete and specific. Not all of them will appeal to every reader. But it's a good list to refer to when we are rocked by rough waters.

Chapter 5

Rethinking Forgiveness

IN 2006, A man with a gun walked into a one-room schoolhouse in a small Amish community in Pennsylvania and shot ten girls. The next day, Amish neighbors stated that they forgave the shooter and reached out to comfort his family. Like many others, I thought, *How can they forgive so quickly and completely? Are they just mouthing the piety they've been taught, or do they truly believe that?* I could not imagine forgiving someone who killed my child.

We are taught to admire those who forgive, yet it goes against our nature—and common sense. Still, those who vow they will get revenge don't seem very wise. Revenge begets more revenge, just as violence spurs on more violence.

This is a tough question without easy answers. It sparks controversy and debate. Not everyone has experienced a crime, but many of us know the feeling of a hurt that festers. We're tempted to lash back, yet that usually makes things worse. But easy forgiveness just gives someone a free pass on bad behavior, doesn't it? So what do we do when anger and hurt feelings boil up inside us?

THE QUESTION

Can we truly forgive? If so, how?

Pamela

I have a philosophy about forgiveness. I don't think forgetting is necessarily part of it. But forgiving allows you to let go of what that person has done to you. It's a sadly familiar story: Somebody kills a child and goes to jail for murder. The mother says, "I forgive him." But of course, she can never forget. What she does in saying that is let go of what this guy has done to hurt her. Then she can be freer to move on.

I'm sure there are a lot of people who can't forgive. But if you don't, the anger festers in your heart, your mind, and your body. It's there all the time. That keeps you upset. It might not come quickly, but over time, if you can give that away, and forgive, then you can move on.

Ruth

Because of the generous, wonderful life I have had, I haven't had a lot of instances of having to forgive. I was adored by my parents and blessed with a lot of supportive and loving men and women in my life.

But I do have one instance: a workplace relationship that was so devastating to me that I'm still working on forgiveness, years later. This man engaged in behavior that seemed beyond the pale. A large part of it was not what was done to me but what was done to other people.

I think we are called to forgive, as God forgives us. And I haven't quite mastered it. It's just that one thing! It should have happened by now.

Anna

That word "forgiveness" brings up a knot here in my gut. The abuse that happened to me as a child seems beyond forgiveness. I haven't got it all done. Maybe I never will.

Still, I have read a lot on the topic and tried to help others with it, both as a chaplain and as a class leader. One thing I know is that forgiveness is about taking care of oneself, not the other person.

Most often a wrong cannot be undone, and forgiveness gets stuck in somehow trying to undo the wrong. If you insist that forgiveness requires that the wrong be undone and that there be recompense, your attitude keeps you tied to the person who hurt you.

Forgiveness requires grieving first. When a wrong is committed, it creates an up-down relationship between two people: the one who committed the wrong is up and the one who was wronged is down. In the grieving process, there's a balancing and equalizing process. That is to say, the victim is no longer thinking in victim terms. As long as I am that person's victim, I am tied to him. If I let that go, the wrong is still there, it won't go away, but if I don't hang on to that and don't remain a victim, I can begin to become whole again.

Healing needs to happen before forgiveness. It's healing for me if I forgive another person. Also if I've wounded someone else, and I care about whether that person heals, it can be a healing thing for me, too, that I can be forgiven.

In cases of domestic violence, though, it's complicated. I was a teacher and an occasional spokesperson for a center for the prevention of sexual and domestic violence. In order for there to be healing, the abuser has to admit to the abuse. Also, the victim needs to acknowledge that there was abuse. If she doesn't, that's what keeps her there, because the abuser says that it's the victim's fault. She interprets it as "I've been bad" not "I've been abused." There needs to be what Marie Fortune, a minister who founded a center for the prevention of sexual assault, calls "justice making." That involves interaction, learning, growing, and healing. Justice making has to come before there is reconciliation. Sometimes the abuse is such that there can be reconciliation while the couple lives together; most times, she's got to get out of there. In that situation, forgiveness is down the road.

You shouldn't rush into forgiveness. It's never the first thing. So many Christians say, "We must forgive." I say, "Bleh! Like it's your fault!" Old-time pastors used to counsel battered women to "Forgive and forget. Go back home where you belong. Be a good wife." It's sad stuff, and it still happens. It isn't the job of the victim to initiate the process of forgiving the abuser, until she's ready to become separate, no longer tied by the abuse.

Susan

I think we have to remember that God loves us regardless. It's up to us to forgive ourselves to some degree for the stupid things we do. God forgives us, but we have to forgive ourselves and not spend the rest of our life wishing we hadn't done it.

Eva

I know it's not healthy to hold grudges. It's commonly agreed that holding grudges hurts the grudger more than the grudgee. If I hold a grudge and don't attempt to understand why someone did or said whatever—and if I resent that person rather than forgive—it's going to weigh on me more than it will on him or her.

I really try to understand why someone might have done something that didn't seem particularly loving. Sometimes you never come to an understanding, so you just have to let it go.

Jane

I have not been hurt in a personal way that required forgiveness. I pretty much pulled out of issues that might be hurtful to me. But I am sure I have hurt other people by being neglectful, forgetful, or thoughtless. I remember my sister telling me one time about how it hurt when I forgot her birthday.

These days, I find myself trying to keep connections with people, particularly family. Part of it is knowing that we're mortal—that our relationships won't continue forever—and needing to keep that connection as long as possible. Not being in touch is a way of being thoughtless and hurting other people.

Isabelle

I do have trouble with it, but I'm working on it. I can get angry and not show it. One man I know often says things that make me mad. I boil up inside, and I want to speak but don't. I go home and get angry. But sometimes you just have to say to yourself, *It doesn't matter anymore. That's who he is. You have to let him be.*

As you get older, it gets easier because you can see it in a broader picture. You feel like there isn't anything you can do about it anyway. Why let it bother you? It bothers *you*. It doesn't bother *them*. As you get older, it's easier to accept people as they are.

Joy

Forgiving can be extremely difficult, but if you do it, it is totally freeing. To forgive is to love again. It may mean loving somebody who is really hard for you to love. At least in my case, that was true.

I had to forgive someone who knew me as a child, someone very close to my family. He did the unspeakable thing, and if I had told my parents, I thought they wouldn't believe me. I was only ten. I didn't talk about this with anyone for most of my life. I did not know how to handle my feelings and buried them where they remained for years and years. Then as an adult, when I remembered, realized, acknowledged it all, I was conflicted and emotional about it. I knew that the suppression of the memory was hurting me, and I needed to address it. So I began reading about childhood abuse and began thinking about forgiving.

It happened dramatically for me in meditation—nearly fifty years after the fact. Five of us went on a three-day silent meditation weekend, where we promised not to talk to each other, except after dinnertime. I figured that it was a perfect time to deal with this shadow in my past. I took several books with me about the topic of forgiveness. I read and read. I thought it would happen easily, but it didn't. On the last day, during the last of many meditation periods, I gave up, figuring it was not going to happen.

I remember sitting in a rocking chair, and I had a vision of a butterfly that flew across a wide field where sheep were grazing. I "followed" the butterfly as it flew over to a little yellow flower. Somehow I knew in my heart that the fragile flower symbolized the man I needed to forgive. I felt overwhelmed by peace. Then, with this beautiful pastoral image in my head and heart, I became aware of tears streaming down my cheek. That's when I knew what was happening. I felt washed with forgiveness. I had totally let it go. I was a new person.

It made me realize what a burden I was carrying by keeping such pain inside. I had never spoken about it to anyone in my family because I knew that it would have damaged my relationship with this man and his family. They would have denied it. Or I would have angered them. It would have been hurtful to everybody, and it wouldn't have helped me at all. Maybe that seems like weakness— to forgive and not have the whole world know what a terrible thing somebody did. But I have learned from the example of Jesus, and my faith, about forgiveness.

MY TAKEAWAYS

I'm fortunate that I haven't had much suffering in my life. But forgiveness is not only for those who have experienced crime or abuse. Perhaps you've had a terrible argument with your friend, where she said some unforgivably mean things. Perhaps a close relative has cut you off for months or years after a big blow-up. Perhaps you still get worked up when you recall the nasty way someone treated you or someone you love. That person may be living in blissful ignorance of your bitterness. Yet it still eats away at you.

After listening to these wise women, what I learned was that the point of forgiving is not to let the perpetrator off the hook; you forgive because you need to let go of past hurts in order to move on with your life. You forgive in order to free yourself.

Another takeaway is that forgiveness is about taking care of yourself. If someone says or does something terrible to me, I need to think twice and not lash back. If I can prevent it from happening again, I will. But when possible, I need to convince myself to let it go. I don't have to have the last word; in fact, the one who insists on having the last word is the smaller person. And I can choose not to use up my emotional energy on hating that person for what he or she did. Likewise, as Susan says, sometimes it's better to forgive yourself and not let regret strangle you.

Chapter 6

Redirecting at Midlife

ONE REMARKABLE THING about these nine women is that all embarked on new directions at midlife. Two did so reluctantly, because of divorce, but found new passions to guide them in the second half of life. Most of the others took deliberate actions and created a new self-identity after the age of fifty.

For women especially, midlife can be an exciting time for new adventures. For mothers, it is a time when children leave the nest. Women who haven't had a job sometimes begin to work full time in some area they once dreamed of—or find work of a type they never imagined. Those who have spent decades in one field sometimes quit their jobs and embark on new endeavors, perhaps volunteer work for a cause. Full of energy, minds roiling with new ideas, some women go back to school for further education.

For me, it was a switch from journalism to book writing. I had spent fifteen years as a journalist, working for *Business Week* as an editor and a correspondent. At the young age of twenty-eight, I achieved my dream job: Hong Kong bureau chief, covering China at a pivotal time in its history. After eight years of loving that work, I might have gone back to New York to climb the ladder and become a high-level editor. But instead I chose to switch to an earlier dream I had imagined from my girlhood days: becoming an author. It was a rocky transition. But I hit my stride in my fifties, becoming highly productive and creating book after book.

The transition to new directions can be thrilling, but it often involves setbacks and requires deep reflection. Our identity changes in the process, and that can be wrenching. It may cause us to ask questions about ourselves: If I am not a full-time mother, who am I? If I am not a teacher, who am I?

Each of us has a different path and a different sense of how we might redirect our lives. Still, I find it motivating to hear how these women made it through their midlife transitions.

THE QUESTION

What choices did you make at midlife to move in new directions? How do you make a meaningful life for yourself after retirement and/or empty nest?

Pamela

For six years, when my children were young teenagers, our family lived on a farm in a rural area near my husband's family. It was twenty-five miles from the nearest town, very isolated. For a while, I had a job working as a foster-parent adviser, but the drive was very long. I didn't do farm work, but I was very busy keeping the house and raising the children. Life got more difficult as they entered their teen years.

I was deeply depressed by the time we moved back to our suburban home around 1985. I tried to do some kind of work other than teaching. I took a career-interests test, and the results said I was most suited to teaching, especially preschool. Still, I took a job with a company that sold pagers and beepers. It was a disaster. I got fired because I wasn't any good at it. I did some home-chore work for older people for a while and then reluctantly agreed to teach three-year-olds two mornings a week at a preschool newly set up by my church. That preschool was very small, and I liked the other teachers, also members of my church.

Then one day, when I was in my late forties, I really surprised myself. On the last day of school one year, the director came by each classroom and said, "This is my last day. I'm going to retire." We were all speechless. All the extroverts *and* the introverts were speechless. After she was gone, we didn't know what to do.

Although I was one of the newest teachers at that time, I suggested to the other teachers that we get together and talk about our options. That seemed logical to me because nobody knew what to do. When we got together, we looked at each other. I said, "I think we need to decide, first of all, do we want to continue the school or should we close the doors?" You can't go on unless you have a plan.

All of the teachers (there were six in those days) said, "Oh, we can't close it. We can't!" Then somebody said, "We need a new director." We all looked at each other, and I said, "I think I can do that." I was surprised to hear myself say that. I mean, what was I getting myself into? I had no idea how to be a director.

That was in the spring, and school was just out, so we had to figure out how to get ready for school in the fall. We were running with half the children that we could serve, so it was a rebuilding job. We just took one thing at a time. We made decisions, and everybody pitched in. I set up a school board, and we made up some bylaws. It was such a grassroots, exciting time to be in a position like that.

That was in 1986. I was director of that preschool for eighteen years.

At first, we had less than thirty kids, ages three through five. Each year, we would add a few more students, and within five years, we grew to being full with a waiting list. I took the phone calls from parents. I talked to everybody and gave them the rundown. I tend to be an idea person, and I usually like the ideas that I come up with, but I'm also flexible.

Every year, we added to our numbers, and we began a class for two-year-olds. By the time I retired, the school was averaging more than seventy-six students in seven classes. That helps one's self-esteem to be able to do that. Yes, I liked that.

Anna

It's real common, particularly when the kids are grown, to think, *Now who am I?*

The commitment a mother has to make, with the constancy of childcare, requires all of life. How women work full time with kids at home, I have no idea. I don't know that I could have done that with five kids. My husband and I both believed it was best for me to be home with the kids. Not that we had any abundance at all. We skimped and saved, just barely keeping above the poverty line at times. But I was there with the children. I didn't want somebody else to raise my kids.

Once they're grown, you think, *who am I now?* For some women, it's very hard because they don't feel they have permission to break loose and be something new. For others it's this great opportunity, providing that it works out in the marriage.

Fear was huge when I first started seminary, at the age of fifty-two. It was hard to concentrate. I couldn't read a page without thinking about what the family needed or what was going on or who was doing what, because with five children who are very close in age you develop this constant awareness of someone else, not yourself.

Learning to focus was a gift. I learned that I *can* do theology—that in fact, I do it well when I focus on it. I know how to think, which I'd never realized before.

Jane

When I retired from teaching, at about sixty, I was all geared up to do things like serve as chair of the ecumenical church council of our city and work with the presbytery on various committees. I slid into retirement because I cut down my hours before I retired from teaching. The school had taken on a new head who wasn't working out too well, and it was a good time for me to leave.

By then, I had already geared up to several of these other activities. I had these connections, and I had served on boards and so on; I loved doing that and working with people who were really inspiring. I've served on the Pittsburgh Theological Seminary Board for six years. Then I was offered a position on the advisory board for the School of Theology and Ministry for Seattle University. After many years serving on committees at the presbytery level, I served as moderator for one year. Later I served on a national committee of the Presbyterian Church considering the issue of ordination of gays and lesbians. All of these appointments had church connections that I had been fostering for some time. It was like a second career for me.

When I stopped teaching, I also became a volunteer chaplain at an inner-city hospital. That was an important development; listening to other people in change mode helped me get through my own changes. I learned a lot about myself. In order to give pastoral care to someone else, you have to reflect on your own life. Perhaps that made a big difference in how I got through life changes later on. This did force me to be more self-reflective.

I learned to intentionally develop personal relationships, with boundaries, but with openness at the same time. It helped me see myself without so much self-criticism, and I also realized that you can relate to people without being critical. You can be with people who aren't perfect. You can have a relationship without fixing them.

Joy

Just before I turned fifty, the kids were finishing their schooling and leaving home. I had been involved in church and community affairs ad infinitum. It was a great time to hold my life up to the mirror and examine it. What have I done, and what am I going to do? I did not know where that would take me, but it felt adventurous.

I decided to expose myself to things that I had rejected doing earlier in life—for example, math. It was time to challenge myself with difficult intellectual stuff, and not do just good things in response to what other people were asking me to do. To be proactive on my own behalf! That was the idea.

First I enrolled in a remedial math class at the university. I have never felt competent in math, so this is where I began. It was a humbling start, but very good in the end to confront my worst weakness.

The second thing I did was join a women's investment club, and thirty years later, we are still going strong. I have learned a great deal, and now I manage my own investments and follow the markets daily. This was an excellent decision for me.

Next I decided to study for a master's degree that would expand my horizons. I chose an unusual master's degree program offered by San Francisco Theological Seminary. I asked two friends to write recommendations for me, and they became enamored of the program and enrolled also. One of them was Susan, and we went through the four-year program together, earning a "Master of Arts in Human Values," a unique program designed by the seminary particularly for laypersons. Among our classmates were teachers, writers, and people in social justice or nursing careers.

This was an external degree program, which meant the professors came to our city, and each month our group spent an entire weekend in classes, after a month of studying and reading and writing papers. At the conclusion of our coursework, we had to write a thesis. My topic was "creativity and women." It was a hugely enriching program for me. I interviewed fifty-five women in many fields of creative work, including the arts, science, business, and education, and wrote about their values and conflicts.

Shortly after graduation, I was invited to apply to be a member of the newest committee of the national church, an advocacy team that examined issues concerning women. This fit beautifully with my concern for recognition of women's full participation at all levels of the church. Later, I was asked to serve on a national committee about ethical investing. I could speak up about issues that mattered to me, and I got to attend several meetings a year, all over the country.

This began a whole new phase of my life, earning my master's degree and moving into the national church.

Katherine

When I was in my forties, I was invited to do consulting. I learned on the job, reading like mad, trying to understand what my colleagues were talking about. I felt like I was tiptoeing along and there were huge gaps of ignorance that I might fall in. I knew that I needed a stronger base in theory. If others took my advice seriously, I needed to take myself seriously, too. So I went to graduate school. My younger child had just gone to college, so I had an empty nest. It was a two-year program.

I studied organizational development. This led me more deeply into organizational development in my practice. I was working for a consulting firm whose practice originally was partly labor and partly personnel.

After I finished, and while I was in graduate school, I did a whole lot more in this field for the consulting firm. It was great because I'd be learning this stuff, and I could go right out and start using it with clients. One of the two partners whose names were on the door was very interested in this as well, so I was teaching him. He was a compensation specialist, but he was interested in this new specialty, organizational development. All of a sudden we were doing new things, such as increasing participation in organizations and quality circles. We were expanding the practice of the business. I was having a wonderful time.

Then they asked me to be a partner in the consulting firm. Here I was at midlife. Talk about your ego being stroked! It was an honor. All the partners were men. I thought it would be so cool to be the first woman partner. Then I listened to the way they talked about their lives. They would sit around and say "ha ha" to how many weeks it had been since they had a weekend with their families. It started to make me very sick to my stomach—literally.

In the beginning of my daughter's sophomore year, I was in graduate school and all of this was going on. We took my parents to visit her at college, and we drove around New England. We celebrated her birthday, and all of that night I was sick. I could not get out of the bathroom. The next day my husband said, "We're supposed to be flying home today." But I was too sick to get on a plane. He called the airline and they said the only way I could cancel my reservation on that flight and get a refund was if I was so sick I had to go to the hospital. I said, "If I have to get up off this floor and get dressed to go anywhere, I'm going to go home."

I managed to fly home, and then my husband had to go out of town. I just continued being sick, and by the end of the week I was so dehydrated I wasn't making any sense. One of my chosen sisters came over and said, "I'm calling your doctor." I went to the hospital. I had "diarrhea of unknown origin." They tested me for everything. I just had a bug.

I finally came home with my Pepto-Bismol routine, every two hours whether I thought I needed it or not. It gave me time off from work. And I thought, *This is not about my body; this is about my spirit.* Then I got healthy and went back to work. I continued on the same path and finished the two-year academic program, and they were still asking me to become the firm's first female partner. In the meantime, I had a hysterectomy. That made me take more time off, so I had more time to think. I finally realized that something was wrong with this whole scenario.

That's when I went to see Alene Moris, a leader in education of women for leadership roles. I asked her, "What's wrong with me? I have this great opportunity, and yet I'm in the midst of the same fight I've been having my whole life. Here's my head telling me one thing, and here's my gut acting up." It's only later in life that I began to tell myself, *Oh, my gut is telling me something. Stop right there and pay attention.* I've been great at ignoring my gut and listening to my head.

I listened to some of my women friends who knew what I was talking about. Women do have a different way of approaching things, and honoring your family is part of it. They said, "Of course, you don't want a job that requires you to work eighty hours a week. You will make a ton of money but have no time for anything other than work. There's nothing wrong with you." Oh, duh! I had been going through a process of denial, trying to put myself into the mold that says, "This is what success looks like."

Finally I realized that being a partner was not for me. As soon as I got it, I said to myself, *There's got to be another definition of success.* So I started my own consulting firm, and I got to choose my own hours.

At midlife, you do get these intimations of what's true and real for you. They may not have anything to do with the path you thought you were on. Some people can say, "This possibility is coming in, and I trust it and I'm going this way." Not me. I've got to fight it for a long time. I finally got there.

For me, the other midlife thing was to stop being a good wife who dutifully followed her husband everywhere and continued to try to do all the housework. That was just a killer: the fight to say to my husband, "Let's reorder the roles and responsibilities around here." Ben is a flaming extrovert. He's very affable and sure of himself, and if he has an opinion, it comes right out immediately. I'm more of an introvert, which means I've got to get inside and try to figure it out before I'm sure enough to say anything. So it was easier, and it worked better for him as well as me, to just go along with whatever ideas he had.

The midlife thing for me was starting to honor *me*, to stick up for what I thought at home as well as anywhere else. I wasn't graceful at it, because I wasn't very well practiced. It wasn't gracefully received all the time because it was a big shock. It had to happen or I would've died. Some of this stuff you just have to do, or you're going to wind up being namby-pamby your whole entire life—and who wants that? I wanted to have a life.

For some of us, there's a cosmic two-by-four that hits you over the head. But some people never get that. I had some good friends who have pretty much stayed in line and not made waves. I think that's a shame.

Isabelle

When the children are grown, you say, "Okay, now who am I?" I was somebody's mother wherever I went. I think it has to do with the children; it also has to do with growing. Also I think it has to do with men because there was a shift in Sam. He was the dad for our two older children, but he stepped it up and took a lot more care of the youngest than he had the others. He would even take her to nursery school before he'd go to work. I think he had changed. He's always been very supportive of me; whatever I did was just fine— the acting and all that.

If you are having a life change and you want to do something else, it helps to have a husband to talk it over with who's very supportive of you.

Eva

At the time that my husband gave up on our marriage, our sons had left the nest, and my only brother and my parents had died. Yet in spite of the sorrow, gradually, all kinds of interesting opportunities began to occupy my time and my mind.

One of those interests is Dudley Carter, a local artist known internationally for his monumental Native American-style wood carving. Just before I met Dudley, I had spent years going to and from Canada to help my parents through numerous health issues that compromised their golden years. (I am eternally grateful for Canada's universal health-care system!) After my parents died, I had a "conversation with God" asking what I might do to make use of the experience I'd had dealing with the challenges facing old people. *But please, God, don't make me go into another nursing home!* I thought.

An amazing thing happened. A most remarkable old person came into my life. Dudley Carter was 99 years of age, very wise, very vigorous, but at a point in his life where he could use a little help carrying out his sculpture business. Now I'm no sculptor and Dudley had plenty of apprentice sculptors at work with him, but my rather limited basic skill set seemed to fulfill other needs creeping into his life. I figured Dudley, one of the most youthful people I had ever known, would live out the 120-year life span prescribed in Genesis. I also figured that I could spend time helping out a bit around the studio, acting as his secretary, doing some typing for him, and watching the wonderful art take shape. And I did—for a short time. Dudley died in 1992 just a month shy of his 101st birthday.

I learned so much from that man. His life and his art were indeed inspirational, so following his death a friend and I set to work on a book about him. We interviewed numerous people who knew him in the art world and beyond and gathered stories and photographs, which should turn into a fine book someday.

Another interest came in a roundabout way in 1996. I was living on my own, and my old abode was becoming a fixer-upper. I was given the names of three contractors to interview. One was Jihad. He and his presentation stood out, so I hired him. Jihad had a sweet way about him, and after he'd been working around the house for a while, I felt comfortable enough to say, "Based on your name, I figure you must be a Muslim." I knew next to nothing about Islam. Jihad told me that yes, he was Muslim, but he had grown up in a Catholic family in South Central Los Angeles. He explained that he didn't find the self-discipline he needed and got into some trouble as a young man. Eventually he found true Islam, and there he found the guidance he felt he needed. He said he took the name "Jihad," an Arabic word that means "struggle for God," because, he explained, his "whole life has been a struggle for God."

Jihad piqued my interest in this other faith. I told him that I'd never seen a Qur'an and asked if I could buy one. He said, "No," so

I figured you have to be Muslim to have a Qur'an. But then Jihad said, "I can give you one." Sure enough, he brought me a Qur'an, which he had lovingly inscribed. He said he also had a little card he wished to give me, but he'd forgotten to bring it. I anticipated that it might convey some wise words from Mohammad or the Qur'an, but when he finally gave it to me, it turned out to be a quotation from Proverbs: "A friend loves at all times." The text went on to define a friend: "A friend is one who knows who you are, understands where you've been, accepts what you've become, and still, gently, invites you to grow." I treasure that little card, its message, and the kindly messenger who gave it to me. I figure that if Islam is leading Jihad to be the gentle man I came to know, there must be considerable goodness in it.

Then, when the horrific acts of 9/11 occurred, I was concerned about Jihad. I wondered, and I still wonder, how life would be for him having the name Jihad. I tried to contact him but couldn't find him, so I still don't know where he is or what he is doing. I wish him peace— *salaam*!

Because of 9/11 and having met Jihad, I wanted to know more about Islam. A mosque in my city held an open house and that is where I met Farida, a woman who is a wonderful ambassador for peace and understanding. Envisioning greater opportunities for dialogue than could be had at her mosque where men and women could not meet together, Farida became the driving force behind a series of interfaith fairs. We held the first fair at our local community college in 2003. It was so encouraging to be a part of those fairs. No proselytizing. Only generous, gracious sharing of understandings. I met many interesting, involved, and concerned people who have opened my mind and helped me to understand and appreciate other faiths, other beliefs—even my own faith in a broader context.

I think friendly conversation elevates our collective consciousness and expands our wisdom. Wisdom cannot be contained. No one human being or one group of human beings can claim, at this point in our evolutionary transformation, to have it all. I think wisdom is something we cannot possess, but it can flow into us—especially if we are in good company. I like a thought attributed to Sir Isaac Newton, "God, grant me the company of those who seek the truth, and God, deliver me from those who have found it."

Nowadays I find no end to opportunities to engage in interfaith and cross-cultural exchanges with people who seek truth and strive to grow in understanding. I suppose we have 9/11 to thank for that development.

Susan

At midlife, I went on and got my master's degree. The kids were near the end of their educational years. The youngest was finishing high school. Going back to school for a master's was wonderful because I thought I'd lost the ability to think. After raising children you just think, *Oh, for heaven's sake. Do I only know how to bake cookies and serve tea and wash diapers?* It was wonderful to be able to write and read again. We had to turn in papers every month and read two or three books every month. I was very grateful that my husband was supportive.

I got my master's degree from San Francisco Theological Seminary. I started in 1978, when I was in my mid-forties, and I graduated in 1982. My thesis was on a sustainable lifestyle. It was a good experience.

Ruth

I was a typical 1950s housewife. I had no desire to work, at all. I loved being at home. I had not particularly been a "child" person, but I loved and enjoyed our children. And I loved my husband. I would have been totally happy to stay at home my entire life, or so I thought!

My first husband, Tom, was a sweet, outstanding young man. He had started college at Stanford and later switched to a smaller college, where I met him. After we married, he went to Yale Divinity

School and received a Master of Divinity degree. He enjoyed it, but he realized he wanted to go back into forestry. He spent many years in the Forest Service. During Nixon's presidency, with the cutbacks, he got what seemed to be, and was, a wonderful opportunity: to work at a large forestry company as their manager of educator relations. He was able to do some exciting things in environmental education, which was his love.

But during a middle-management layoff, he lost his job. It was horrible for him. He was never then able to get back into his field. Even before he lost his job, Tom's behavior had begun to change. Unbeknownst to any of us, he had been at risk for Huntington's and he was showing its first indications. We thought it was severe depression from being laid off and not being able to find work. We didn't know what was going on; we didn't know that he was ill. It was, of course, most painful for Tom, but the rest of us didn't know what we were doing either! When a diagnosis was finally made years later, it was, along with being frightening, a healing time for him because his relationship with his kids and with me had become frayed.

By that time, I had taken a job in the office at a church that was near to our home and would allow me still to be available for my ten-year old daughter, Sara. We had almost no income. One of our sons was in college, and we had one child left at home. I truly did not know whether I would be able to support her.

My work experience at that church ended up being positive for me. It shored me up, partly because I was surrounded by community and people who cared about us. One of many pieces of grace during this time was that a band of people in that community helped—mostly anonymously—to put Sara through college. And I learned that I could support myself and my child. That made me feel very strong, self-reliant, and in control of my life. That's what was missing for so many women, early on in the 1950s.

The forties and fifties of life are absolutely a time of opportunity, of fresh starts. Those years can be a wonderful new beginning for women.

MY TAKEAWAYS

The strength these women showed, facing serious challenges at midlife, fills me with awe. A "fresh start" is not always welcome. Sometimes it grows out of depression or loss. And it may come with severe diarrhea!

Sometimes, it means being open to things that flow your way—and acting on them. After her divorce, Eva had no idea what was coming next. She didn't have to volunteer to be a wood sculptor's assistant or write a book about him. And she didn't have to strike up a conversation with a worker at her house or help her Muslim friend organize interfaith fairs. One thing led to another, and she chose to follow the path as it revealed itself. "Wisdom is something we can tap into—if we're in good company."

But for others, it is important to be proactive. Joy deliberately set out to explore things she was not good at, including math and financial investing. Her midlife study of both investing and women's issues qualified her for positions of national prominence within her church.

Yet others set off with fervor, only to realize it wasn't quite right. Katherine set about acquiring the education she needed but then found she didn't want the plum job that was offered to her. That realization came with a gut-twisting illness and hit her like a two-by-four. "At midlife, you do get these intimations of what's real and true for you. They may not have anything to do with the path you thought you were on."

Whether your way is reactive or proactive, finding out you can be "strong and self-reliant" matters. So does "self-reflection" and "listening to other people who are in change mode." Also, it's important to have "a lot of guts." Sometimes you have to tiptoe, if you're going against another's wishes. But, like Pamela, you may surprise yourself.

The most hopeful comments I heard, though, are these words

from Katherine:

"I think that the fifties are a remarkable decade for women. Maybe because the kids are off to college or gone, and you've decided what your strengths are. You have this period where you are still very vital, sought after, respected. I've watched many of my friends blossom and come into their own in their fifties."

Chapter 7

Finding Your Calling

I **WANTED TO INCLUDE** a question about work since it takes up so much of our time and our mind-space. But I hesitated at first because of generational differences. Women who came of age in the 1950s and early 1960s faced social expectations that they should place marriage and family needs first. When young, they were told they had only a few work options, and they lost those jobs if they became pregnant. Most spent years as housewives. Those of us who came of age in the 1970s or 1980s expected to have careers, and we eagerly jumped into fields previously dominated by men. So what insights could our elders offer us about work?

Because of this generational tension, I struggled to find the right way to word this question. "Finding your calling" might seem too grandiose; perhaps "choosing the right work" would be a clearer way to word it.

As for me, I was career driven from an early age. My parents assumed that their three daughters would get a college education and then follow their husbands, but when my older sisters were in college, my dad realized that social expectations were changing. He belatedly gave my sisters advice on jobs and then turned his attention to me. Noting my interest in writing, he helped me get a summer internship with the local newspaper. From then on, I avidly pursued a career in journalism, hoping to combine it with my interest in foreign languages. It wasn't until years later, though, that I identified how my work reflected one of my core values: building bridges of understanding between Americans and people of other countries. In my case, my work helped shape those values.

I decided to ask these wise women not only about their work choices but about how those choices reflect their core values. Work can be about more than making money; it can give our lives a deeper meaning that feels more like a "calling."

THE QUESTION

What choices have you made about work (whether paid or volunteer) and how does that reflect your core values? What advice would you give others about finding their calling during early adulthood and at midlife?

Katherine

I don't know if it's "calling" or "purpose" or "self." I think it is terribly important to discover who you are, what your particular skills and gifts are, and how you can use them out in the world. It's a matter of stewardship, really: returning a portion of what you've been given to make the world a little better. This is especially important for women.

In my generation, we spent way too much time conforming to society's expectations and too little time discovering who we were born to be. I can't tell you how many conversations I've had with women who are struggling with questions like "Who am I?" "What do I have to offer the world now that my children are about to leave home?" "How do I move out into the world and matter now?"

Work and career added great meaning to my life when I got around to them in midlife. I loved being a wife and mother, and I always had one outside volunteer commitment that I cared about.

But it was really cool to be a consultant and realize that when I went somewhere as just me, not so-and-so's wife or so-and-so's mother, people felt I had something to offer that was valuable to them. That was life-affirming to me, and I believe that sort of experience is affirming for anyone.

I wonder if women in their forties and fifties can relate to those of us who went from full-time homemaker with volunteer commitments to career woman later in life. So many young women, including my daughter and daughter-in-law, had careers before marriage and children. Some of us have envied that your generation seemed to find your calling or vocation earlier than we did, while we did what was expected and then had to discern if there was a calling that was singing to us when we got to or near the empty-nest stage.

I remember my daughter saying to me, "I'm not going to do it like you did, Mom."

"What do you mean?" I asked.

"I mean I'm not going from college right into marriage without finding who I am first."

I knew what she meant, and I thought that very wise at the time.

Pamela

I studied to be a teacher. In my days, science and mathematics were not ever mentioned for girls. I had several aunties who were teachers, and it seemed like that might be the right thing to do. It turned out to be right for me.

When my kids were teenagers, I tried other kinds of work. I hadn't renewed my teacher's certificate, so I couldn't get a job in the public schools. I did home-chore work for older people. I soon found out that wasn't my calling. However over the years, I have found a place inside me that feels comfortable with older people. I might be led in that direction.

When I got involved with early childhood education, I knew it was a calling. I loved it. I absolutely felt comfortable there. I couldn't get enough. That lasted me the whole eighteen years. Sometimes it was hard for me to get up in the morning because of depression. But when I got to the school, the kids would inspire me. I could carry that through the whole day.

I found that I had some leadership skills in working with adults, with the teachers. Also, I was able to come up with ideas and look at the whole picture. I felt good about my work as director of the preschool.

If someone asked me for advice, I would say, "What do you like to do? What makes you feel successful?" When I was teaching, sometimes parents would send me the nicest notes about how happy their children were at our preschool. Raising children, I had learned that I don't need external validation. Still, those notes made me feel like I was doing something important.

Since retiring, I've been struggling to find my calling for the next phase of life. I've considered watercolor painting and photography. I have a friend who is going to start working for the public schools as a tutor in the classroom. I'm going to explore that, try it and see.

What I'm finding out now is that a person's calling changes. What was working for me ten years ago isn't working for me anymore. I didn't realize it was going to be this difficult for me.

Really, I like retirement. But I need to have something more—to fill that empty space.

Joy

When I was a young mother, in the late 1950s and 1960s, my life was centered on my family, faith, and community. After I finished teaching, my family consumed most of my time and energy, without a doubt. My work was supporting my husband with whatever was needed and taking care of the kids so he didn't have to. This was the way it was for most women at that time in America: wives = homemakers, husbands = workers. We think of these attitudes as sexist now, but in the 1950s we were unconscious of that. If we thought of it at all, our "job" was to manage the home and family, and then to contribute to the community.

Then as the kids got older, I thought, *What am I going to do with all that coming free time?* I decided I would go back and get a master's degree, but I didn't know in what. Answering that question was really fun.

In high school and college, I enjoyed writing and had continued that interest with my community work. I knew that what I would end up doing would include writing, but I didn't know how. I also enjoyed reading about and discussing theology with a small diverse group from our church. For many years, three other couples came to our house at six in the morning once a week for breakfast, prayer, and dialogue. Our pastor and leaders gave us difficult books to read, and we thoroughly enjoyed discussing theology. So I wasn't afraid of studying that.

In the end, I found a special program that met on the weekends for a Master of Arts in Human Values. It dealt with religion and community and was very broad. I took classes for three years through a seminary and a local university.

At the conclusion, I had to write a thesis. I thought, *What do I really want to research? What can I contribute that has not been studied before?* I wanted to understand more about creativity, in particular how creative women managed to produce in spite of obstacles. So I interviewed fifty-five creative women and asked very specific questions to try to understand what creativity meant to them, what their values were, and how they resolved their conflicts. Their responses were absolutely fascinating.

I interviewed artists of many different kinds: an architect, a weaver, a painter, a teacher. I talked to a journalist, a novelist, and a short-story writer. I met with a piano teacher, a singer, and a composer. Because I was traveling with my husband for his work, I could ask people all over the country. When we went to New York, I found a woman who was writing opera. I talked to doctors and scientists. I even interviewed a nun and a rock star. Hardly anyone said no when I told them I was doing a thesis on creative women, their values and conflicts. They wanted to talk with me about it. What I did validated women, and many of them told me they made changes in their lives because of the probing questions we considered.

Writing about creativity was enormously fulfilling for me. I learned what my personal questions are and what the answers would be for me. I learned how others dealt with conflict. For example I learned that the best way to write was to "put the critic in the closet, and let the writing flow."

I admired how these women were comfortable in ambiguity and even cherished an openness to possibility. That's where they got their abundant energy. So I began practicing that in my life. I also began to understand feminism and the challenges it provoked in our culture. And I began applying all these principles that I was learning to my church work.

So I would give this advice: Think about what you really love. You'll always be happy if you're doing what you love—even if you think you can't do it. Don't be afraid to try something new. What is there to be afraid of?

Absolutely reach out for what you're passionate about. I would never have dreamed that I could have been in the places where I ended up.

Jane

I'm a bookish person. School has been a very high priority in my life. A lot of energy went into the things I studied in high school and college and graduate school. I identify with academia. I felt the need to be a teacher, to be in the classroom.

My mother was an office manager for my father's business for many years. Later in her life, after Mother had to leave the family business, she did more studying and became a children's librarian. Her mother had been a librarian, too. I think perhaps I was influenced by both my mother and grandmother—although I wasn't intentionally trying to mimic their patterns.

But why a biology teacher? I just had a natural delight in how living things worked, people and animals and plants. Also, I spent a lot of time outdoors, hiking and skiing. Even in high school, I was considering medical school. That would have been a high-achievement badge, to be able to go to medical school. I applied but wasn't accepted, so I did graduate work in zoology.

I think I would like to have been male. In the 1940s, who had the opportunity to do things? Men did. I grew up at a time when boys were valued for things that I valued. In high school, I definitely felt I was competing with boys. Partially, it was because I saw that typical women's work wasn't valued. It's only later in my life that I began to value what my paternal grandmother did. She was an incredible gardener, housekeeper, and cook, and she raised nine children. But I didn't want to do that. I wanted to be good at math and science. I wanted to do what the boys could do. They got acclaim. That has popped up at other times in my life—competing with what the men could do.

After I retired from teaching, I wanted to be more involved with nature causes. I applied to sit on a local land and water use committee. I did stream monitoring, bird-watching, and butterfly catching.

Then I also became more active in ecumenical organizations. I was interested not only in my own denomination but also in other denominations and how they worked together. What appealed to me was the breaking down of barriers. I felt it enriched my own spiritual life to be in touch with people who had come through different traditions. It was good for me to know that the Spirit was moving beyond my own church and that we could work together.

Anna

When my parents died, and when my husband's parents died, I witnessed that all four of them seemed unfulfilled. I thought, *I am not going to do that. I am going to be somebody.* I had no idea what that meant.

My mother was a very highly educated woman who could have

taught high school math, English, and French, but she never did. My dad didn't like his job. He didn't know how to speak up for himself. It seemed to me that he longed for something but didn't know what it was.

When I was at home raising my children, I had, off and on, thought it would be interesting to work as a chaplain, as a volunteer. Two or three times I went to do it, but I realized I wasn't ready. Our youngest son had major surgery when he was just six years old. I was at the hospital with him, and that environment was appealing to me.

Later, a pastor helped me to realize more of what was inside me. We had talks about theology, and he had Bible studies that opened my eyes to progressive Christianity.

I remember one time talking on the phone with a woman I admired and saying, "If I had it to do over again, I might go to seminary." She said, "I understand. I might, too." When we were younger, that had not been a possibility for either of us. I had grown up Episcopalian, and it was many years before that church allowed women to be ordained. For a long time, I thought, *Maybe*. But I wasn't of an emotional stability to be able to go to seminary.

The call to ministry was one that built over time. I was always active in the church, whatever church I was in. Over the years, I gradually become more and more interested in theology and leadership, especially leadership.

Then a seminary opened up in Seattle. And all of a sudden, I inherited another $10,000 from my mother—money I wasn't expecting. I said to myself, *Now there's a seminary in town. Does this mean I have to put my money where my mouth is and do it?* It was very frightening to take a class for credit after thirty years.

While I was taking classes, I didn't know for sure what I was going to do. Toward the end, I did an internship at a hospital as a chaplain. It was like *Yes! That's it!*

I found out that that's who I am—a chaplain. Not "I am hired as a chaplain." For me it is a ministry, which is there whether I'm being paid for it or not.

I found out by doing it. Often, I would go back to my office and say, "That worked." It felt right. Working as a hospital chaplain was rewarding and a great privilege.

As for advice, I would say it depends on your circumstances. If you are hard-pressed for funds, you don't get to have much choice. The important thing is when you do have spare time, do what nurtures you. Find the joy, where you can give yourself a gift, whether it's poetry or volunteering or learning a new language—something that is fulfilling for yourself. That is a part of self-care at any time. Maybe you'll find a new path for yourself. Just keep looking.

Eva

I've been really lucky. Not knowing exactly where I was going, I ended up in jobs I loved, even though they weren't what I had in mind.

At the age of sixteen, I began working in a department store because that's where I could get a job. It was fun to be around the merchandise and see what's new. I was a "floating contingent," but mostly I worked in the boys' department. The manager there was a delightful person; he really enjoyed his job. I decided I wanted to be a buyer, like him.

I went to the Chamberlain School of Retailing in Boston, and part of our job training was to work in a department store for the six weeks before Christmas. I got to be a floor manager at Jordan Marsh. Buyers I worked with there seemed tough and crude. They would get on the phone and swear at the manufacturers. I figured I couldn't do that.

So I decided I'd really like to go into personnel work. After two years at school, I was lucky enough to get into the executive training program at Jordan Marsh. The director of our school advised us, "If you want to go into a department store, apply for a job in merchandising because that's where the most opportunities are." I told Jordan's I wanted personnel, and I got it! I was really happy I didn't take the director's advice. Sometimes you just have to follow your own intuition or your heart's desire.

In the personnel department, my primary role was training sales people, but my boss said she would also like me to supervise the training of the elevator operators. She asked me if I liked "colored people." I told her, "I've never met one I didn't like." Actually, I hadn't met many, growing up in Calgary. At Jordan Marsh, the elevator operators were all black. At that time, that was a choice job for black women in Boston. My main concern about taking on the responsibility was that I didn't know how to operate an elevator, but someone else trained them in that. My job was to teach a class called Starring You that focused on courtesy and personal appearance. It was a class we also taught the sales people. Can you imagine that class today?

I just loved working with the elevator operators. Most of them were a lot older than I was. I was twenty-one at the time, and they were all mothers and grandmothers. I didn't have to teach them anything about courtesy because they were the most courteous women you'd ever hope to meet. They were polite enough not to mind me going through the steps with them. Again, this job was nothing I would ever seek out. I'm sure I learned much more from those wonderful women than I ever taught them.

After the two-year executive training program, I went back to Calgary. There, I fell into a job in advertising, and I found that I really liked that. That was just an accident. Whether good fortune or divine intervention, it was something I couldn't have planned.

I wanted to go back into personnel work, but I couldn't find a job in that. A department store had an ad in the paper for a proofreader, and I landed that job. They hired me to be a proofreader, but the very first day they had me writing advertising copy! I did that for about three years, and I loved working with all those creative people. The boss was brilliant, and the artists and the display makers were really fun. I would pound out some words, and a few days later they'd be in the newspaper! It wasn't something that I ever imagined I was up to.

After I married, I didn't work outside the home until years later, when our kids were older. Then I got a part-time job at a title insurance company, proofreading. That was really a rut. Job conditions were bad—nowhere to grow, no "attagirls," no feeling you were doing a good job. Plus, all of the typists smoked. I came home every day with a headache. After about a year, I quit.

Working there made me realize it's so much better to have a job you enjoy where you feel you can grow. If you can find work that satisfies you and that you feel is going to benefit others—that is the ideal. Just this morning, somebody sent me an e-mail that said, "The only difference between a rut and a grave is the dimensions." Some people work only for the money—and of course, they have to have the money, so they're stuck. Or they're doing it for the benefits the company gives them. It's a real blessing if you can have a job you enjoy.

In recent years, I have been standing with a group of Women in Black every Saturday, handing out flyers on the street and talking about the need for peace. I prepare many of the flyers myself and enjoy talking with total strangers about this. Looking back on jobs that I've had in the past, I wonder if I was being prepared for this point in my life. Sales work helps you interact with people you don't know. In personnel training, you help other people interact with people they don't know. I learned to do a little advertising work, which helps me prepare these flyers. Spreading the idea that peace is a real possibility is probably the most important advertising work that I could do. I think, *Thank you, God, for putting me in those positions that I might never have tried.*

Isabelle

Most of the theater acting I did was not paid. But in recent years, I've done a lot of commercial acting, and it's really fun.

When I moved here, I got an agent. She is a charming lady and very good. I had to audition for her. She has found me lots of jobs.

The biggest, by far, is a series of ads for the local transit authority. I also did a commercial for Taco Time, and I did a wonderful movie about Alzheimer's for the Department of Veterans Affairs. That was a really big job because it went on for several weeks. I have also done a lot of in-house health videos for hospitals and nursing homes.

A big software company flew me to New York City to spend a whole week in a loft where they had set up different rooms with computers. I was in the kitchen demonstrating what computers could do there. Every day, different people would come through, including journalists and people from other countries. After that, they sent me to Las Vegas for the electronics show. One year, I was demonstrating a little kitchen computer. This is me, who can hardly work a computer! The second year, I demonstrated a camera that could take a picture and put it on your computer. That was a fiasco. People would come by and I couldn't make it work!

Besides getting paid, what I love most about commercial work is the people. They're all young and very eager. They love doing it. I don't know if it's because I'm old, but they are very solicitous and kind. I just love being with them. It gives me hope for the world because these people care about what they are doing. It isn't about the money; it's about creating something.

More and more, I think that creativity is all-important in life. I love watching my little grandson as he creates artwork. Nobody tells him what to do. That's the saving grace of life— being able to create something. I love being around people who are able to create something. In a way, I'm creating something too, a character. That's how it reflects my values.

Here's my advice: Go after your gut feeling and do what you really want to do. It isn't always possible. It isn't always lucrative. You do have to balance how you're going to support yourself and how you're going to create. Maybe you have to do some job you don't like to earn money to do something else that you do like. But somehow find what you enjoy—even if it's only volunteer work—and if you really want it, go after it.

MY TAKEAWAYS

It's interesting to me how many of these "nonworking" women ended up with careers. Only two started adult life with a career and one of those stopped working when she had kids. And yet many of them found out that once the kids were older they still had a lot of energy and discovered, to their amazement, that there weren't that many barriers in their way at all.

Because the women I interviewed didn't have to work, they represent only part of a generation—but an interesting one. For them, work was an option for fulfillment, and they went for it. It seems they benefited from the way times had changed over the twenty years between when they had kids and when they were empty nesters open to new things. They may have thought they were forgoing careers for children but, in the end, they didn't. Career post-children wasn't necessarily taken on with a huge sense of ambition, but it became quite fulfilling.

Their stories show how early dreams change over time. Many of these women began adult life accepting that their true calling was raising children. But later they formed new dreams—and achieved those, too. This clicks with a belief I hold: Life has many seasons. If you prioritize raising children during one season of your life, it doesn't mean you can't find fulfilling work in another.

I love Joy's idea of interviewing a bunch of women you admire and asking them tough questions. Obviously, that's what I've done with this book. Listening to other people's experiences is a great way to learn.

Feeling like you're successful not only feeds your ego but makes you feel like you're doing something important. Those handwritten notes Pamela received from parents are gold. I hope she gets them out and looks at them sometimes during her retirement. Whatever your initial hopes were, positive feedback is what makes work satisfying.

The work you do is right if you feel comfortable, at home, inspired, appreciated, and creative. If you can't get enough of it, if you discover skills you didn't realize you had, if it fills your soul, then it's the work you were meant to do—your calling.

Until then, just keep looking. Take risks. Maybe you'll find a new path for yourself. And fulfill a new dream.

Chapter 8

Raising Teenagers

MY COUSIN LIZ loved the years when her kids were teenagers, and she devoted her working life to helping troubled teens in an alternative school. But, in my experience, she is an exception. Most parents I know cringe when their children first start rolling their eyes with annoyance—around age twelve—and hang on for dear life through the years of rebellion and defiance. A friend once told me it seemed like an alien inhabited her daughter's body during those years. Then we breathe a sigh of relief when the alien departs, and our young-adult children delight us anew.

I have to admit I'm in the majority on this one. My daughter was sweet and thoughtful as a little girl and really not so bad as a teen. But she insisted on staying out far later at night than I thought safe, and we had some confrontations that I'm hoping to forget one of these days. By her early twenties, she stopped telling us how much she resented us, and now she even enjoys spending her vacation time with us. My sweet and thoughtful daughter has returned.

The dilemma, as I see it, is this: Teenagers want their parents to let go, to free them up to make their own decisions, even if they make mistakes. Of course, they need to differentiate from their parents and find out who they are as individuals. But an essential part of being a parent is providing guidance, and parents know from their own teenaged years that this is a time when bad decisions can sometimes lead to dire consequences. How do you balance the desire to provide guidance with the need to let go?

If there's one slice of wisdom I'd grab for quickest, it's insight on how to raise teenagers. Many of my friends are convinced they made mistakes, and I know I did. What deep truths should I have held onto while I was dealing with those raging hormones?

THE QUESTION

What did you learn about parenting when your kids were teenagers? What advice could you give to somebody else who's going through a rough time?

Isabelle

My children all did horrendous things. Sandra ran away from home. Mark was just a loose cannon. I'm sure they did marijuana and drank and who knows what else. Annie was even in an alcoholic recovery unit. So all of my children had very volatile teenage years.

I always told people, "There's a person in there and they come out of it—if you're lucky." They're pulling away from you; they're trying to figure out where their life is and how they fit in this society. I always wondered, because Mark and Sandra were adopted, if they felt more so that they didn't know who they were, so they had to pull away to find out.

Most children go through this time when you think they don't like you. But they do, and they come out of it.

Just be patient. Try to figure it out. It's painful. When I see people who have teenagers who don't do all these things, I think, *Wow! That must be wonderful.* Of course, at the time, I thought they were better parents. I thought I was a terrible parent. It depends how deeply they get into drugs.

You just have to be there and let them know you love them even though they are doing terrible things and making you feel like a very bad parent. You do have to love them. I know that sounds sort of trite, but in a way it isn't. If you truly care about them, you want to figure out what's happening. You love *them*, just not *what they're doing*. Some parents take very extreme measures. I think you have to just be there for them. I don't know. It wasn't a fun time.

A lot of it has to do with watching your own children and what direction they've taken. If you say to them, "Well, that's really interesting"—without judging—then you may find out more, even though the direction they took doesn't have anything to do with what you would perceive as the right way to go. If you can get through that, it can really be fun. Some people just don't approve of their children doing what they do, and that's a shame.

People have said I was very lenient, and I was. I don't know how they all came out of it, but they did. It was very hard on our marriage. When Sandra ran away with some friends and stole our car—that was the hardest time. Sam felt it as a betrayal. Then what you're dealing with is your spouse's feelings. I didn't want him to hurt as badly as I was hurting.

Just trusting teenagers doesn't work. But they do have to try out things; that's the meaning of being a teenager. It's like a two-and three-year-old. They are pulling away from you. They are finding out who they are. That's why they are so rebellious at two and three. They think, *I'm doing this on my own. I have got to find out how I work.* That's how teenagers are.

Their friends say, "This is something you might enjoy. This is fun." Of course, they're going to try drugs nowadays. I don't know how we handled that. We were just oblivious, maybe. We always said, "Call us. We'll come and get you." I guess I've forgotten a lot because I wanted to.

We moved our youngest, Annie, when she was in the middle of seventh grade. You should never move a teenager in the middle of the seventh grade! We moved from Mississippi to Oregon. She had a lot of trouble at first. It was hard. Then she went into a drug rehabilitation place, though not for long. She shouldn't have been there anyway. After she came out, I always trusted her. Later, she got involved in the drama club in high school, and she's still friends with all of them. They were wonderful girls, and they were always at my house. I did trust her then, completely. But she had gone through the hard part. I remember finding birth control pills as I was going through something. She was on birth control and she hadn't told me. I just told her that I thought she was smart to do that, but I wish she had told me. So you find out your children are having sex, in high school—and they do!

We always took a lot of kids into our house who were having troubles with their parents. Once, when Sam was gone in Southeast Asia, I decided to go on a trip with a friend. I actually left Annie alone in the house, in high school, with this guy, Tim, who moved in with us because of trouble with his parents. I left them there, and it worked out fine. I said they couldn't drink. Evidently, he brought some liquor in the house, and she kicked him out and he left. I did trust her. Actually, I trusted her most of the time.

Joy

Everyone knows how important it is to love your children. That's easy to do when everything is going well. But when things don't go so well, it is even *more important* to love them. That is when it is most difficult to be a parent. The worse they are, the more you need to love them and affirm them. I remember gritting my teeth at times when I needed to be a loving parent, when I would rather have screamed at the kid.

I had a friend whom I admired and respected for the way she was raising her children. She once told me, "You are going to be finished raising your children by the time they are age twelve." I was astonished. She explained, "By then you've taught them everything they need to know about having a relationship with God, being honest and kind, and being a good friend. These are the things you teach during preschool and primary years. By the time they are in high school, they know it. Your job now is to trust them and let them know that you trust them. If you do, they probably won't disappoint you." I liked this philosophy. And it worked out for us for the most part. Maybe we were lucky. We had no big problems with any of our kids.

A teacher entrusted our eldest, Carol, to be the captain of the school patrol when she was barely ten years old, and it made a lasting impression on her. She came home from school that day and told me with grave concern that Mr. Ahern had appointed her to be captain, and that she was to select the other kids who would be on the patrol. Her classmates and friends were badgering her to choose them. And she believed that some of them should not be chosen. "What do I do, Mom? They are my friends and they are asking me!" I told her that if Mr. Ahern thought she was capable of selecting the right kids, then she was. I also suggested that she could ask him about those that she had concerns about, and he would probably help. The amazing end of this little story is that seven years later, when Carol was writing her very important college entrance applications, she had to write about a significant person in her education, so she wrote about her fourth grade teacher. When I asked why she chose him, she said he taught her about leadership because he trusted her. This little essay helped her get into a top-rated university.

But trusting doesn't always work. Our son, James, wanted to start up a greenhouse so much that he talked about nothing else. He had developed an interest in growing plants in the sixth grade and seemed to have a true green thumb in our garden. So his dad helped him build a marvelous greenhouse on our south-facing deck. We watched him plant all sorts of seeds and care for the fledgling plants. One day someone broke in and stole his plants. He didn't know how to tell us because it was a guy from his school, and the plants were marijuana. Well that was when the plantings in the greenhouse received much more supervision! James went on other business ventures in high school, from his own acrylics design business to a party service, and he later became a financial consultant for retirement portfolios of major national organizations.

Advice? Love them like crazy, even when—and especially when—they seem "unlovable," and trust them not to disappoint you.

Katherine

We were very tied in with our church and the youth group. In those years, the youth group at our church was huge. Most of our very good friends were members of the church, and we had all done stuff with our kids, so they knew each other pretty darn well. I always thought that was part of why they had a relatively sane and safe teenage time.

We had two very, very different kids. Jed acted like the first child: his philosophy was "Show me the carrots, the rewards, and I will work my little tail off to reach the rewards." He was always a good boy. Of course, now I hear he did all kinds of stuff in high school that we had no idea about. He was smart enough to keep it from us. He was involved in sports. He was in the first class of Natural Helpers. In his high school, Natural Helpers was a club of students that were identified as good listeners, and they gave them some training and identified them throughout the school as peers you could talk to if you had problems. He was the kind of kid that would be selected, and he acquired those skills.

Kelly was two years younger than her brother, and her attitude was "He's the athlete. I'm not going to be the athlete. He's this, I'm not going to be that." She had a group of friends who were like her, very bright and a little bit young, socially—if not a lot young, socially. Jed was in the popular group, and Kelly was in the not-popular group. Her friends were a lot more interesting than Jed's friends, but very different. They would dress up and go to *The Rocky Horror Picture Show*—stuff like that.

Kelly was very bright and always did well in school. So by the time she was in eighth grade, she had taken all the classes to be in ninth grade. She was in junior high, and they wanted her to go to the high school and start taking classes. We were thinking, *She's an October baby. She's already a year younger than a lot of people in her class.* That's because they started school in Illinois, where it was a different age cutoff. It just seemed like the wrong move. So we looked around, and she fell in love with a private school for the arts and humanities. It was in its first year, so she went there for a couple of years. Then she said, "Okay, now I'm ready to come back," so she returned to our local high school.

When she was fourteen, she was just awful and we were the dumbest people on earth. You never knew who was going to come out of her room in the morning. It was dreadful, to the point that we all went into counseling as a family. The counselor said, "Count your blessings that she is doing this and being so disagreeable. You love her so much. If she wasn't disagreeable at this point, you would never be able to let her grow up." Then the counselor looked at Kelly and said, "You count your blessings too. If your parents weren't such jerks, you would never be able to pull yourself apart from them and grow up." Then he told us all, "So this is perfect, what's happening. Here are some rules for how you can all talk to each other in family meetings." We learned those skills and exercised them.

I remember the year she was fourteen was just the year from hell. By the time Kelly came back to the high school, she had enough of her own legs under her that she didn't need to be obnoxious. She had found singing and joined a local girls' choir. She had found her own place.

What did I learn? Let them be who they are. They were very different. There was no trying to make her be like her brother. There was no pressuring him to take her along so that she could learn how to be cool. When they went to college and even beyond, it was like one was the yuppie and one was granola. To a certain extent they're still like that. They're very good friends now, which is lovely.

There's one other thing we did, and I would credit my husband with this. Somewhere along the line, Ben said, "We need to have money for these kids to go to college," so he set up mutual funds through the Uniform Gifts to Minors Act. I think we gave $600 a year, maybe it was more, for Jed and for Kelly. By the time they were ready to go to college, there was enough money so that they could pay their way anywhere they wanted to go. Then Ben turned it over to them when they turned eighteen. People were aghast. He said, "These kids know what this money is for. They've never done anything that leads us to think they aren't trustworthy. They can handle it." And they did. They paid their college tuition and graduate school.

This shows the level of trust that Ben had in those kids all along. He always had a great time with them. He trusted them and thought they were funny, capable, and smart, and they lived up to it.

Ruth

Both of our sons were teenagers during that really difficult time, the 1960s and the 1970s, when many young people were getting into drugs. We thought we were going to be lucky because we had the kind of family where we *thought* everything right was in place. To an extent that was true, but there was some experimentation with pot and alcohol—enough to make us aware and more attentive.

All three of our kids were good students and involved with us in our church community. Neither Tom nor I were strict rule people. For good or ill, who knows? They are each now responsible, loving, happily married adults and bring continuing joy to my life.

Eva

In my family of origin, our father was the disciplinarian. He let us know what was expected, and we knew if we didn't do what we were expected to do, he would be the one to take care of it. Dad had been a captain in the Canadian artillery and expected my brother and me to obey like good little soldiers. Fortunately, we had a mother who always managed to smooth things over. As a teenager, I confided to my mother that I didn't think Dad loved me because he was so strict. My ever-loving mom explained that "Your father is strict with you because he loves you so much." I came to understand and appreciate that when I had children of my own.

Since Mom was the tenderhearted parent, I figured that when I became a mother that would be my role. It didn't turn out that way. My kids' dad had many good points, but he just didn't have it in him to be a disciplinarian. I had to be "the heavy." I had to set the goals and the rules and follow through on them. That was tough; I didn't like it. I couldn't simply say, "Just wait until your father gets home." I often found myself yelling in order to get attention. In spite of my inept disciplining, by the grace of God, our sons turned out surprisingly well—super dads—both of them.

When the boys were little, I had a spanking spoon—kept it on top of the fridge. I used it sparingly, maybe a time or two. Usually, I'd just have to walk over to the fridge and the young gents would get the message and stop what they knew they ought not to be doing. That may work with little ones, but you can't threaten teenagers with a spanking spoon. When they became teens, I yelled some and prayed lots!

I am exceedingly grateful that we didn't have any major problems with our kids. We were lucky! Blessed? I thought that raising teenage boys was a challenge, but looking back, our experience wasn't anything compared with what many families go through.

Jane

I don't know if I have any advice. Somehow we did get through. We tried to balance requirements with freedom. In some cases we did better than others, but I can't even give you a prescription of how we did this. It was so much on a case-by-case basis. Sometimes of course it depended upon what was happening with us, the parents, at that moment. We tried to balance protectiveness with letting go and encouraging freedom. We like the result.

I can't think of any overall change we would've made. We really didn't have any strict rules, except things like "Let us know where you are." I am encouraged that our three daughters are good friends now. They weren't always good friends.

Pamela

We took foster children in for a while, and they were all teenagers. They didn't give us foster children who were the same age as our own, so we had teenaged boys in the house before our own kids were teenagers. Still, that experience was different than dealing with my own teenagers, later. They taught me humbleness!

I had to work on patience. There's always the question: How much is nurture and how much is nature? I preferred to think it's mostly nurture. I thought that we would have quite a bit of control as parents—and we did have some. Yet when it comes right down to it, you can throw in some guidance, but you have to accept them for who they are, not what you want them to be. That goes back to nature.

And it may not be what you expect. All of our kids turned out differently than I thought they would. I had to go from "I think my children should be President of the United States" to "I just hope they're good citizens." It came as a relief to know that I didn't have to fix them. I just had to nurture who they were and try to guide them. They didn't like it very much, and they didn't always do what I asked them to do. But over the years they have said, "We had a good childhood" and "Thank you, Mom, for being a good mom."

In the teenage years especially—I guess all throughout the parenting—there's this balance between letting go and guiding. As a parent, you're supposed to guide, but there's always this tension with the need to let go. In the teenage years, you're changing that balance the whole time.

In all my years of teaching and foster parenting, I had quite a lot of experience with other people's children, so I observed when parents were trying to be dominant and trying to get their kids to do what they wanted them to do. I could see that that just wasn't working. Basically, you just have to live your own life doing what you think is right so that your children see it. They won't show that they see it until later, and you may have to wait a long time for external validation.

When it came time for our son to graduate from high school, he needed to do something, but he didn't know what he wanted to do. We realized that he was a very good mechanic, even in his young years. So we encouraged him to go to community college for that strength that he had—with the idea that if he didn't want to do it later, he didn't have to; it was just the next step.

It was the same for all three of them. Our older daughter could grow anything. She had a green thumb like her grandmother and her dad. So that was kind of a no-brainer. She did go to college for one year, but she decided it wasn't the place for her. Then she went into horticulture and sailed through. That was her passion and still is.

Our younger daughter didn't know what she wanted to do. She didn't want our advice. I'd go to bed crying a lot because she just was so awful to us. She had finished high school and she didn't want any more school. On a particularly bad day, she said, "Mom, I just don't know what to do!" She was crying and miserable. I said, "You've always loved to comb hair and fix hair." And she did—she always loved playing with her dolly's hair. "If you were to go to school to learn how to cut hair, you wouldn't have to do it forever, but it would give you a focus now." At that point, she was so low that she agreed to do it. She finished the class and graduated, and she just loved it and did well. Turns out, she's a good chemist with color! It gave her something to focus on, and she was able to get a job and earn good money. For a while, she even had her own salon.

My highest priority for myself was my family and taking care of them, and I didn't always do the best job. I was an absolutely outstanding mother for young children. I lost it a little bit when they were teenagers. It was frustrating, and we went through some pretty bad times. That certainly strengthens you.

Susan

I remember that between ages thirteen and eighteen my children were difficult. We made some mistakes, there's no question. I wish we could go back and change them, but we can't. We did the best we could with the knowledge we had, and that's what we go back to, again and again.

You can beat yourself up, endlessly asking, *Why didn't I do this?* or *Why didn't I do that?* and haul around the "backpack of guilt." But you don't need to do that. You try to make decisions with the best part of you, with the knowledge that you have and the experiences that you have, with the money you have and the time you have, and the situation you find yourself. If you try your best, then you shouldn't beat yourself up. As a parent, you're not trying to alter someone's life negatively, you're just doing the best you can.

Every kid is so different, and so is every situation. Raising children in today's world is not like raising children thirty years ago. Any advice that I would give now would have to be tempered by what is happening in today's world. We didn't have the prevalence of drugs; there was some alcohol, but nothing like it is now. We didn't have the fear factor of somebody abducting our kids.

I guess more than anything, good parenting means doing things with your kids, trying to understand them, supporting them, but helping them to be realistic about what they can or cannot do because of who each child is. The only thing you can really do is try to believe in your kids, help them to learn what's destructive, and help them to learn how to make good choices. Remember the saying, "Life is choices. Make good ones." Help them learn how to weigh things.

One of the things we often said to our boys was "I *love* you and care for you, but I don't *like* what you are doing." There is a difference between "love" and "like," and what they mean to those with whom we engage. Also, we stressed the importance of honesty, even when that is painful, both for the teller and the receiver. What has been ultimately important to us is family, the support we can give each other, our kids, and our extended family.

As we grow older, all we can do is live each day, reach out to those around us, and believe that our children have worth. How do you teach your kids that they are worthy? I think it's by believing in them.

MY TAKEAWAYS

Obviously, there are no easy answers. Every parent has a different experience, in part because every kid is different. I guess no parent can get through those teenaged years without making mistakes.

How's this for variety?

+ "Your job now is to trust them and to let them know that you trust them."

+ "Just trusting doesn't work."

+ "We had no big problems with any of our kids."

+ "My kids all did horrendous things."

+ "I'd go to bed crying a lot because she just was so awful to us."

+ "I had to work on patience."

+ "Somehow we did get through, and we tried to balance requirements with freedom."

+ "I thought that we did have quite a bit of control, as parents. And we do have some. But when it comes right down to it, you have to accept them for who they are, not what you want them to be."

+ "If you try your best, then you can't beat yourself up."

+ "It came as a relief to know that I didn't have to fix them. I just had to nurture who they were and try to guide them."

+ "When parents try to be dominant, it doesn't work. Basically, you just have to live your own life doing what you think is right so that your children see it."

+ "We made some mistakes, there's no question. I wish we could go back and change them, but we can't. We did the best we could with the knowledge we had."

On the surface, none of this is reassuring. Oddly enough, though, I find some reassurance here. These are women I find to be very wise. Yet many of them had trouble with their teenagers and admit to making mistakes, too. Even the one who raised foster children and spent her life educating other people's children. You raise the children you're given—not the ones you wish you were given.

I made mistakes. My child turned out fine. It seems that's the best any parent can hope for.

Chapter 9

Relating to Adult Children

WHEN MY DAUGHTER was growing up, I had an addiction to self-help books. During pregnancy, I read *What to Expect When You're Expecting*. Then I read baby books, *Parents* magazine, and every book I could find on toddlers, shyness, cultural literacy for children, step-parenting, and of course, raising teenagers. But have you ever noticed that there aren't how-to books on relating to adult children? Why is it that, when our kids are grown, we parents get no more advice?

My husband has two children from an earlier marriage, so I had adult children even while my daughter was small. From watching him, I learned early that relating to adult children has its challenges. If you believe what your friends write in their annual Christmas letters, you would think this is never a problem. But if you sit those same friends down with a glass of wine, you'll realize that it is.

The problem centers on what I call "guidance" or "advice"—what adult children call "nagging" or "meddling." During the growing-up years, parents take on the responsibility of guiding their children, and it feels unnatural—wrong, even—to suddenly stop caring what happens to your kids when they become adults. You brought them into this world; aren't you responsible for them? You want them to be happy, and when you see them marrying the wrong girl or making a bad financial decision, you want to point this out to them so they can avoid the pitfalls of life. Somehow, this concern gets twisted, and they see you as the bad guy. They hear the message that you think they can never do anything right. They hear the message that you're blaming them. If they show you some work they are proud of, they want your praise and encouragement. If you offer the slightest bit of advice on how to improve it, they think you're tearing them down.

Do I sound like I know what I'm talking about? I suspect most parents with grown children have struggled with this at some point.

So what's the secret? Some parents get along just fine with their adult children. Is it luck of the draw? Easygoing personalities? Or is it good parenting decisions?

THE QUESTION

How do you manage your relationship with your grown children?

Ruth

I think it's terribly important not to get hung up on trying to be too involved in their lives. Yes, those lives may not be all that I would have imagined for them, but it is gratifying and fascinating to see through the years the lives they have chosen for themselves and their children. My instinctual advice would be "hands off!" My kids tease me about the fact that if they receive a "real" letter from me, it is serious business. There have been, I believe, two of those in their adult lives, and it *was* serious business!

As for my daughter, I have been very careful to avoid treading on her life. Her brothers were gone by the time she turned ten. It was just she and I living at home until she left for college, and we are very sensitive to each other. We talk about a lot of things and share some of our feelings, but on certain issues, I try not to probe too deeply.

Along with encouraging decision making early on in children's lives, I would say the key is to keep your mouth shut!

Katherine

You just bite your tongue. The biggest thing I would say about my young-adult children is this: If they ask me for advice, which they rarely do, I will give it. If they don't ask me for advice, I don't.

I think you have to keep your mouth shut and just be encouraging, encouraging, encouraging. I remember how insecure I was at times—even about the way I decorated the house or how the kids were behaving. I remember whenever either my mother or my mother-in-law said something encouraging. It's really important.

My mother-in-law never offered advice. But if you asked her advice, she would give it to you with both barrels. You didn't ask unless you were really ready, because if you asked, she would tell you, in words of one syllable, exactly what she thought. But she was very careful and supportive and fair.

There's another piece with your young-adult children. You can relax and be a little more human than you were. As a parent, you had to be the great role model and act as if none of these thoughts doubts and worries never entered your mind. When you're vulnerable, you end up being closer to them. And chances are the kids can take it. If you want to share something sensitive with them, chances are they might have expected it all along anyway. Also, they don't fall apart.

I also ask my kids for advice. My son, Jed, is very astute financially, and he knows a lot about the stock market. I have often asked him for advice. He just lays it out very carefully. Recently he got a new job that requires him to build a team of people from all over the world, literally. He said, "I need some help with this. I don't know how to do this." Both Ben and I, being consultants who had done this sort of team-building work, were able to give him some ideas.

Isabelle

I was thinking about adult children last weekend when I was at my college reunion. Three of my women friends told us their sons weren't speaking to them. I found that fascinating because my son calls me all the time.

My children are all kind to me now. I don't know why. I wish I did.

You hang in there with them. You listen to them, if they want to talk to you—which sometimes they won't. If they don't want to talk to you, what can you do? Not much, except tell them, "I love you. I'm here. I care about what's happening to you." But sometimes kids can talk to other people better than they can talk to their moms.

It's not good to give them advice unless they ask for it. If they ask for it, you say, "This is my opinion" or "You might try this." But once they're grown you can't say, "I don't think it's a good idea for you to go out with this guy" or "I don't like this apartment" or "I don't think that's a good job to take." You can't say that to adult children.

You have to be accepting. Once they're grown, I don't see what else you can do. They don't want to hear your disapproval, especially of their spouses. My daughter Sandra has a different husband now, but the one she had before—I wanted to tell her to get rid of him. I never said anything about it when she was married to him—even though he didn't treat her very well. I said to my other daughter, "I don't like the way he's treating Sandra." But I would never have said that to Sandra because she would have stood up for him. Eventually they got divorced, and now she's married to a man who is very nice to her.

As for my college friend, I know why her son doesn't talk to her. He left his wife and is living with someone else now. The way my friend talked about the woman he is living with wasn't very nice. "She doesn't have an education. She has a terrible daughter with tattoos," my friend said. I wanted to say, "And that's why he's not talking to you!" But I thought it would be too harsh.

Expressing your disapproval is not a good idea. They have made their choices. If you see them going in the wrong direction, I don't know what you can do. You don't advise them on course corrections, not unless they ask. I don't know if my children have ever asked. They don't ask because they're grown-ups now; they go their own way.

In a family, you have to accept everybody for who they are, or it doesn't work. Sometimes it's not easy. If you do that, then you are there for them when they need you.

Annie has done some very dangerous things that have been difficult for me. After she graduated from college, she went to Honduras by herself and stayed for about a month. She stayed in people's houses. I didn't know where she was. She'd call and say, "I'm taking scuba diving lessons. They're really cheap." That's scary. She does some dangerous things that I would have stopped her from doing, but I knew I couldn't stop her. Sometimes I fear for her. That's hard.

Kids. They're always with you, let me tell you. Even when they are adults, and they have children and grandchildren.

Anna

It's in their hands, that's one thing I know. I was a pretty controlling mom, doing my best to be Amazing Anna, the Marvelous Mother. Canning and gardening and sewing and PTA and scouts and sewing on badges and making lunches and all the supermom stuff, the whole shebang. It's a good thing I had five children because if I had raised just two, they would have really been smothered—not mothered but smothered.

I think it's partly the kids' job and partly the parents' job to help them be separate. The kids have to define their own independence. But because I didn't have a self, I wasn't very good at helping them have a self.

Now each of them is choosing how to be in a relationship with me. My five children are all different, so my relationship with each one is really quite different. There's love there, for sure, with all of them, and caring, but generally speaking, it's also "Keep your distance, Mom!" They've been making me let go.

Joy

My adult kids are taking care of me now, just as I did for them when they were young, and they act as if they aren't going out of their way. They are all very busy professionals, but they call and they invite me over, or they check in by e-mail or phone. Two of them live on the East Coast. I visit them about twice a year, and they come to see me once a year. The third lives locally, which is wonderful. Having adult children who are loving back—that is a most amazing, incredible gift.

I don't know what the key is…Yes, I do! Love and acceptance. You love them just as they are. After all, they are half you and half your spouse, just with the genes rearranged into an original person. Doesn't God make wonderful stuff?

When Jeff died, the kids "divided me up," although I don't really need much help, at least not yet. Carol, the doctor, handles medical questions and answers; James, the monetary wizard, helps me with financial decisions. And Elizabeth takes care of all the rest, whatever that means. A businesswoman, she is a great problem solver and communicator, among other things. So it is a good arrangement.

I feel like all that unconditional love we gave them for the first twenty-some years when they lived at home is coming back to me in double measure now.

Susan

Learn how to listen. You can't solve their problems, but you can listen. If you let them talk enough, they solve their own problems. Let's face it, that's what a good counselor does. All you can be to your adult children is a good counselor who listens a lot. More than anything, it's really, really important to be there, to be enough of a friend to your kids so that they can come to you and you can listen to them.

They don't really want your solutions. They want their own solutions, but they have to figure them out by voicing their concerns and considering all of the options that are before them. As they go on and on about whatever they are talking about, solutions begin to emerge.

If they ask you, "What do you think about such-and-such?" I think the answer should be, "Well, tell me more about the problem." The more they talk, the more they solve their own problems. You can hear them if you are open and aware of what they're going through. But there's no way that you can step into their shoes and solve their problems for them.

I can't tell you how many times one of my sons would call, upset beyond all reason. He would go on and on, and I'd listen and listen. I would say, "Well, keep me posted about all of this." I would worry about it for three days, not hearing from him. Then I'd call and say, "How did that work out?" "Oh, that was just fine. There's no problem now," he'd tell me. It was ancient history, and he had figured it out because he talked and talked about it.

Too often, we think we have the wisdom to solve our kids' problems. We don't. They have the wisdom in themselves if they are listened to and they talk about it enough.

Sometimes what they need is some financial support. That's something else again. Financial support can never be given so that the person feels beholden—ever. For example, one of our sons was in a difficult situation, and we said, "We will give you x number of dollars. Pay it back into your kids' college fund." Another of our kids needed something, and we said, "Look, we've done this for your brother in different ways. It's coming out of your inheritance. We realize this needs to be done now, in order to overcome a particular situation, but it's 'even Steven,' so don't worry about that."

Each son was different, and they had to be handled differently. But too often we think if we give one child something then the other child has to have the same thing. It doesn't always work that way. Sometimes life is not fair.

More than anything, we have to help our kids to believe in themselves.

Eva

I consider it a blessing that my children have become mature and thoughtful adults. Did I ever appreciate their support when I was separating from their dad! I may not have made it through without their care and understanding. I recognize now that they, too, needed care and understanding through that experience. I hope I didn't make it too difficult for them.

I'm still learning from my kids. Our younger son has always been unusually understanding and a good communicator, even when he was in grade school. He has grown more so as an adult. I'm one lucky woman in that I have a son who has become a financial advisor. He's doing a good job keeping his mom solvent! Not being particularly financially savvy, I'm relieved that I don't have to worry about that.

Every now and then, I am tempted to give my adult sons advice. That's probably not always a wise thing to do. One son is enduring the difficulties of divorce and even though I've experienced that myself, I really can't advise him. I try to reassure him. I've let him know that I know it hurts terribly, but it won't always hurt so badly. It is going to get better. I encourage him to take good care of himself, eat well, and get plenty of sleep. I wish I could do more. Again, I pray a lot. I admire him so much for the way he's handling a difficult situation and for the way he's committed to being a loving father to his sons. I've mentioned to him that his attitude has been so admirable—even superhuman— and that it's obvious that the grace of God is at work there. His brother is a source of strength for him, too—a good counselor, encouraging him to "stick to the high road."

I'd describe my relationship with my adult children as one of admiration, enjoyment, and appreciation. In addition, they've been right there when I've needed a bit of help dealing with some health issues. I also appreciate that they are very good fathers to my grandsons.

Jane

I'm enjoying their adulthood. Two are living at a distance, and maybe it's easier, although I enjoy their company and their insights into things, and I try to listen to their suggestions.

One daughter is living here in the house with us, and we get suggestions from her. That's been an interesting process. When she first asked if she could move in, we thought, *We can help her that way. Yes, let's do it.* It has turned out to be helpful for us; it has given another voice of interaction. She is physically helpful at times but also gives moral support, for me particularly.

Her sisters on the East Coast are very glad to have her here, keeping track of us. In the last year, as we turned eighty, I've become aware that they all are looking at us and wondering, *How are they doing? What do they need?* We used to care for them, and now they are looking out after us.

I'm surprised having our daughter live with us is working out. Her room is a mess, but that doesn't bother me. We work out our housekeeping, our laundry, and other chores. I definitely feel blessed with the way things worked out.

They really do grow up—and can stay good friends. We are glad to be good friends now.

Pamela

My youngest daughter is a prickly one. When she was twenty-eight, she didn't know what to do with her life. So I suggested that she go to counseling. And she actually did. The counselor suggested, "You need to be on your own." She wasn't living here with us, but she was living in a little house we owned, and she was depending on us a lot. Of course, we helped her. I don't know how you *don't* help them, but we probably added to the problem.

She came up with the idea that she wanted to go off on an adventure. She had a boyfriend who had introduced her to skydiving, and she had enough experience to know that the skydiving community is wonderfully welcoming. She knew somebody in California, so she started her journey there. Her car—a red convertible— was as old as she was. She found herself a little old trailer. She sold many things that she owned. Then, with her cat, she left in her old car, pulling the little trailer. That was a hard day for all of us.

I didn't mind that she went out on her own, but here she was, a young woman with a cute little blonde hairdo in this eye-catching car, pulling this crazy little trailer. She took off, heading down to southern California, and lived in her trailer for a while. She was packing parachutes for skydivers. Well, she soon got tired of that. She went to Wisconsin for the summer, but the skydiving operation there closed down in the winter, so she had to find another place. By then she'd heard about Florida. She waited and waited and waited to get going. By the time she left, she had to drive ahead of a terrible storm, all the way down to Florida. Then we would get the long-distance calls: "Mom, I have a flat tire! I need Dad, my car's having trouble!" But she made it to Florida and lived there in her little trailer for a couple of years.

She was just out there and anything could happen! It turned out that there were a lot of nice people out there, including some nice men, which I was worried about. But she's a feisty, spicy woman, so I guess she took care of herself. Then she fell in love—with a gay guy. There's just no end of surprises.

As a parent, you've got to say, "There isn't anything I can do." I just lost all need to fix my children, all my need to make them like I want them. You've got to accept them for who they are. And you have to love them that way, truly. When things come up, you just be supportive.

So, what have I learned? I learned mostly that you just have to love them unconditionally. That's very hard sometimes. Their dad would fuss and fuss, and I'd say, "There is nothing we can do! We did what we could. They learned what they could from us, and they need to find themselves."

That's another thing I've learned, that we each are responsible for ourselves. No matter how much we may say we want somebody to help us, we really don't. Of course, they taught us that lesson.

MY TAKEAWAYS

As varied as their responses were on the question of raising teenagers, these women are all singing the same tune when it comes to relating to adult children: practice "love and acceptance" and "bite your tongue."

Six of them say they have terrific relationships with their adult children, and two admit to having troubled relations with at least one of their children.

Here's the advice I culled. I think most of the nine would agree.

- Learn how to listen, like a good counselor. Then let them talk till they come up with their own solutions.

- If they ask for advice, give it. If they don't ask for it, don't.

- They don't want our solutions. We don't have the wisdom to solve their problems.

- Sometimes helping your kids is not the right thing to do. We need to lose our need to help them. We have to accept them for who they are.

- We also need to lose our need to make them be the way we want them to be.

- Let go. Try not to be controlling.

- More than anything, we have to help our kids to believe in themselves.

That's it. Pretty straightforward. Putting it into practice, though—that's the hard part.

Chapter 10

Lasting Marriage

COMPARED TO AMERICAN women in general, these nine women have a pretty good record when it comes to lasting marriage. Four are still married to the same man after more than fifty years. Two were recently widowed in their seventies after long, satisfying marriages. Three are divorced, but two of them have happily remarried—one to a man, one to a woman. Only one, whose husband left her for another woman, has remained single. It seems we could learn a lot from them about what it takes to keep a marriage up and running despite the many changes we grow through.

As for me, I'm going on thirty years with my husband, and we have a great relationship. Humor is the key, I'd say. When I'm dissatisfied about something, I let him know, but then I temper my comments with a smile and a humorous aside. He gets it. I'm not a screamer; that helps, too.

In my fifties, though, we had some bumpy times. He traveled a lot for his work, so I developed my own friendships and activities around my work schedule. I enjoyed my independence. Then he retired. Suddenly, he was at home all day, every day, and that was where I did my work. He was eager to spend more time with me, but I had outside commitments and friends. At first, we had to negotiate every lunch appointment and evening meeting. I gave up some activities and cut back on others; he nurtured his own friendships and grew to accept the person I had become. Now we do some things separately and make sure we have plenty of good times together. We've discovered a balance of independence and togetherness that works for us.

Just as midlife is a time of exciting changes and opportunities for women, sometimes those changes cause disruption in the marriage. Anyone who has stayed married for fifty years understands the need for negotiation and compromise.

THE QUESTION

What are some keys to a good, lasting marriage?

Susan

Early in our marriage, my husband and I lived through some tough times where we had to deal with crises among our family and friends. Dave and I learned very early to depend on each other. Our families lived thousands of miles away. We didn't have much money, and we didn't have many friends in each new place. We had to figure out how we could work things out together. I think that's why we have a strong marriage. When you have nobody else, you have to figure out on your own how to overcome crises—whether it's having a baby earlier than expected, bringing somebody into your home, or dealing with a relative who is ill.

I think many times young couples just say, "I can't deal with this." They think it's going to right itself or something will happen that will change it to make it right. Well, I'm sorry, but that's conflict avoidance. You have to deal with it.

I would tell every young wife, "Don't start talking about a serious thing either right before dinnertime or right before bed." That's the wrong time. If you can, the right time is after a good breakfast or lunch. Then you have the rest of the day to work it out. But if you bring it up before you go to bed, somebody doesn't sleep. At night-time, problems always feel deeper and bigger. In the sunlight, they are more the right size.

Here's the other piece of advice I would give: If you really want to make a change, and you know that your spouse doesn't particularly like that change, start talking about it a long time in advance. Plant the seeds, and pretty soon it becomes the other person's decision or the other person's choice.

Don't ever expect your marriage to be perfect, and don't ever expect that 50 percent is enough. You both have to give 100 percent. Don't ever expect the other person to complete you. You must be compete, your spouse must be complete, and then you create another entity that is your marriage. In the unsuccessful marriages I've seen, people expect other people to be what they aren't.

It is very true that people grow and change. If somebody gets stuck and says, "I'm satisfied with what I'm doing," and the other person starts going off in a different direction, that will ruin a marriage faster than anything. You both have to grow in a marriage, and it's good to grow alongside your spouse.

Ruth

I'm hardly an expert on this question, but I have been fortunate that both of my husbands were/are lovely men.

I was married to Tom for twenty-five years. Then I lived alone for twenty-five years before I married Paul. I enjoyed living alone. I fought a second marriage for a long time because of that *and* because I know I'm tricky to live with. But Paul is the right person. He's almost eternally patient.

Of course, the reason for success in marriage is caring—caring enough about the other person to rein yourself in occasionally. It's not easy, as anyone who is married knows. What Paul and I do have is tons of commonality. In the beginning, we knew each other in the context of our church family. Then we have the commonality of our faith, of knowing all the ins and outs of the church, the denomination. And this is very important to us: we are politically and theologically attuned to each other. Also, we both love to read. We love theater. He's learned to love movies. We've got lots going for us. My kids adore him and he them.

Second marriages, I think, are very different. Imagine: we thought that right out of college we would know what we wanted for life! It's amazing the number of good marriages that came out of that time. In a second marriage, you understand yourself and, hopefully, your partner better.

Isabelle

Sam and I were really good friends. I love the theater and I love going to the theater. He would go with me, but sometimes I would go without him. Every year I would go to the Oregon Shakespeare Festival in Ashland. Wherever we were stationed, I always said, "I get to go to Ashland with my friends." That was wonderful of him. It's just the support that we had for each other.

We were so young when we started. I don't think there was ever a time we thought of parting, except during our children's teen-aged years. That was hard on our marriage. But we got through them. I don't know how we did it. We just did.

A lot of it, too, is expectation. In our generation, this was your husband for life. This wasn't something that was just for a few years or that you tried out. This was something you worked at. We lived apart several times. He went to Mississippi for a year before we moved down there. He was sent there to figure out how to win the contract to put sewers in that area. Then once he got the job, he went down there to do it. Later, when Annie was in her senior year of high school, he got transferred to Los Angeles, and he lived there for a year before I joined him. But he'd come home on the weekends.

Both of those times, it helped me to be apart. When we were living in Oregon, I was almost relieved because I was acting in a lot of plays, and I just had to worry about Annie and me and no meals or anything like that. He'd come home and we'd have a wonderful time, and then he would go again.

He was just a nice man. In all ways, he was a kind human being. He never wanted to see injustice. He was easy to live with. He had no big selfish desires. I think that was helpful to all of us because I'm kind of volatile. I came from this family where there was a lot of screaming and yelling. Then I got to know his family, and when they get mad they don't talk to you. That was an "in" to help me understand him.

Anna

I've been married for fifty-seven years, and we've had our ups and downs. What does it take? Oh my gosh, who knows?

Commitment, by both people, that it somehow will last. I call it a dance: one moves and the other has to move to be where the first one is, and vice versa. For a number of years, it worked because everything was built around my husband. Then I had to have therapy to help me see how to keep it going. There were times when I didn't think it was going to last, times when I was going to leave. But I realized the pain of leaving would have been harder than the struggle of staying.

When I went into therapy, my husband couldn't understand it. But I went ahead anyway, and he stopped objecting. I realize now that in any marriage where one person feels like the other person's in charge, it's really the other way around. I was the one that had the power in that family, in the sense of major final decisions. I had much more influence than I ever thought I had.

The key is acceptance, just accepting who he is, even if I don't understand. I learned that I couldn't expect him to be who I wanted him to be. I needed to find out who he is, let him know who I am, and help him to see that. I also had to learn to make choices.

It's really about caring. Now we have a long history together, and it's comfortable to be together. It's a known. One reason I quit working was to be home more with him, because I had been gone so much. I knew he needed it. Also, I quit working because I realized how worn out I was, and I needed to stop pushing like I was. He's just comfortable having me in the house. It's funny. I say, "How do you know I'm in the house, if you're in the garage?" But he says, "I just know you're here."

Katherine

An ingredient of a long marriage is to recognize that the two of you will grow at different rates. At some point, one of the partners will be on a roll, growing, learning, developing at a great pace, and the other may feel he or she has fallen behind. At another time, the other partner will be on the same kind of roll, growing, learning and developing at a pace faster than the other. Rather than being threatened by this, it would be helpful for partners to acknowledge the reality and be interested in what the other is learning—or at least in the fact that he or she *is* on a roll, is learning. Be supportive until things settle in.

Some of that learning and growth is sure to disturb the equilibrium of the established patterns in the marriage. Partners may ask for some things to change based on what they have learned, where they have come to in their own personal growth. Expect it. It's hard to say welcome it because it does threaten the status quo. But don't be dismayed or surprised, and don't use it as an excuse to wonder if the marriage is falling apart. The two people in a fifty-year marriage are probably very different from the persons who stood at the altar fifty years ago—and thank God for that growth. Imagine how many different persons have inhabited your marriage already.

Think of it this way: Life partners are usually worthy adversaries calling us to growth; that's one reason why we chose them.

Eva

I think the best way to preserve marriage is for married people to honor their spouses and their vows. Also, respect is important—following what the Dalai Lama terms the three Rs: respect for self, respect for others, and responsibility for one's own actions. I'd add another R— remembering what we loved about each other when we decided to get married.

Understanding, really understanding each other is also important. I wish that I could have understood my husband better. I wish we could have benefitted from couples counseling, but my husband was not so inclined.

When our sons were in high school, we had some rocky times, and I wondered out loud about the possibility that our family could benefit from counseling. My husband wouldn't consider it. Our younger son, who always had a rather happy-go-lucky attitude, didn't think things were so bad. But our older son said, "I'll go with you, Mom." So he and I went off to a counseling center. After a few sessions in which we gained some helpful communication tips, the counselor didn't think that we had any major problems.

But the experience paid off in the long run. Years later, our older son experienced a major depression, and by the grace of God he remembered our family counseling experience and, on his own, he sought professional counseling. To this day I am grateful to that counseling center.

Pamela

We've been married fifty-two years. It takes commitment—on both sides. It takes the desire to be married to the same person. The bumpy parts will strengthen you for the better parts.

Only once did I even think about leaving. I was really mad at my family. I'm not much of a yeller, but I did yell that day. I went to the bathroom and I just stayed there. I said, "Nobody's helping me. Nobody's doing anything." The kids were in elementary school; this was about them, but it was also about their dad. Everybody heard me, including my husband. Just a few years ago, my daughter told me, "I was so afraid that you were going to leave us that day." I really never went that far because where would I have gone?

Hindsight is a marvelous teacher. When I look back on it, it was probably my own fault that I felt I was being pushed over the edge, because I had the idea that life should be perfect and that I should make it that way. I felt it was my responsibility to make it perfect for the whole family, for everyone. Well, everyone was really happy! Except me!

You can imagine how much laundry and how much mess three children and their friends can make. Oftentimes, they each had a friend or two over. When I fixed dinner, it would often be for the five of us plus two or three.

We both have had a strong commitment to our marriage, but I was terribly frustrated with his approach to family. He can be very aloof. His idea of the little babies was "When they get big enough to talk to me and do things, then I'll kick in." That was very typical of husbands in those days. I didn't think it was unusual, but it just didn't seem right somehow. He was gone a lot. He went to work every day, and he'd often come home for dinner and go back to work or to a meeting. That bothered me. I began going to classes for child rearing, but he didn't want to go.

I did try to change it—nothing drastic—but it didn't work. When we were living on the farm, we were having hard times with our kids. I wanted to go to counseling so badly to see what we could do. But he just couldn't do it. So I went by myself.

All of those experiences have made me stronger and given me more "oomph" to try to figure out how to handle all this stuff. But he's a very loving husband; he will do anything I ask him to.

It's just a matter of adjusting to each stage and age. While he was working, I just decided, *Well, that's how he does it. He can't help it. That's who he is.*

Joy

When I look at how few marriages succeed now, I think finding your love is the most important thing that you can do. I met Jeff in college in 1952. I dated a lot of other guys. In fact, I was pinned to another guy for a while, and I had to have that experience to know that Jeff was the right one for me. He waited for me to come around. By his senior year, I absolutely knew that he was the right person and that we would have an interesting life together. Knowing how unusual my life had been with my family moving around the world, it was important to me that I really respect—not just love, but respect—the person I would choose to spend my life with.

We both changed. As his medical and research career demanded more and more of his time, I had to learn to accept and adapt to that. I filled my time with worthwhile work, and when it was time, went back to school. He had to adapt to an independent-minded woman who was recognizing that the world had treated women unfairly. Back and forth we adapted and changed, and it made for a doubly fascinating life. But from the start, we were committed to unconditional love. This means we did the hard work of loving the differences—and the flaws. Nobody is perfect.

In the 1950s, my generation did not have the sexual freedom that is in our culture today. I don't see that freedom as a positive for young people. It was my experience that if you wait for sex, you get to know the person better before you commit your lives to each other. We truly knew each other, our strengths and our weaknesses. We had not lived together, but we knew everything that we needed to know to be able to commit to a lifetime together. Okay, that concept is fuddy-duddy today. But it worked for us.

Jane

My husband, Richard, and I have definitely been assisted by a security that we've had because of his training and his work over many years. We haven't had serious financial problems. I suppose you could say this is our doing, but this is a gift. It has kept us from severe disagreements.

We've just kept up the love relationship. We've had times when we've been angry with each other but not long periods. Somehow we've been able to work these out. Raising children was a definite stress in our relationship, through teen years and so on. Having that joint responsibility actually acted to keep us going. Also, I've always had my own life. I've been active—working on teaching and then volunteer things. That has helped the relationship.

Who knew, in our twenties, that we would be able stand each other for so long?

MY TAKEAWAYS

Hmm. When you get under the surface of those lovely, long-lasting marriages, you see that they're not all perfect. Looking back with honesty, some women admitted to moments of frustration: husbands who wouldn't help at home, stubborn men who wouldn't take suggestions, times when wives felt pushed over the edge.

Midlife is a particularly dicey time. Several women admitted that when they began to grow and change, their husbands resisted. The men felt threatened when the status quo shifted. Yet others discovered it was important to have your own life, to find alone time, to take time to do what you love.

Everyone seemed to agree on the importance of commitment and expectation that the marriage will last. This gives a long-term perspective to immediate problems.

I enjoyed hearing specific advice, all of it hard-won:

+ Pick the right person and take time to really get to know him before you commit be being life partners. Don't be distracted by the fun of sex too soon.

+ Don't expect your spouse to complete you. You need to complete yourself.

+ Both partners need to give 100 percent.

+ Care enough about the other person to rein yourself in occasionally.

+ Don't start talking about serious issues right before dinner or bed!

+ If you want to make a change, and you know your partner won't like it, start talking about it well in advance, so he can get used to the idea.

+ Realize it's not your responsibility to make life perfect for the whole family.

+ Try to understand how your spouse's personality is different from yours, and work out your conflicts with this in mind. No one is perfect.

+ Don't expect him to conform to your expectations.

+ Recognize that the two of you will grow at different rates, and welcome the change, even when it disrupts the status quo.

+ Cherish the differences.

It's important to remember that there are seasons of life. You can't necessarily "have it all" at once, but you can plan your life so that you have what you need in each season. Midlife can be a season of good health and grown children, when women have the time, the energy, and the independence to break out in new directions.

Late life is more likely to be a season where your own health or your partner's requires different priorities. Consider Anna, who worked as a chaplain for seventeen years but then retired to care for her aging husband. Others in this group of nine are now in the same position, pulling back from the work that thrilled them in their fifties and spending more quiet time with their spouses. Health crises can make late life the hardest time, it's true; but for some, the healthy years of retirement can also be the payoff after driving through the stormy weather during a long marriage.

Chapter 11

Healing Difficult Relationships

OKAY, I ADMIT this is a serious problem of mine. I'm just not very good at figuring out what to say—and what not to say—when someone acts in ways I consider difficult. I realize that people I perceive to be difficult are not necessarily difficult to others in their lives. And, of course, when I get flamed by an accusatory e-mail, clearly *I'm* the difficult one in *that person's* life.

One solution is to give up—to cut off relations. And, as one woman says below, sometimes that's possible and necessary. But sometimes it's not—especially if you're part of the same family. I know several cases where family members have cut each other off, refusing to respond to phone calls or e-mails or have any contact for years on end. That certainly stops the pain in the short term and gives both sides time to calm down and breathe—and perhaps even reflect. But it's a brutal way of dealing with human differences.

For years, my preferred way was avoidance. I would either stay away from the person or try to avoid controversial topics. If I knew someone might blow up, I would just not say what I was thinking. I do believe that some things are better left unsaid; I never bought into the message that we should just let it all hang out and say whatever is on our minds. In fact, it seems that whenever I open up and tell someone honestly what I think, that person ends up angry or hurt. But avoidance isn't terribly effective. I discovered that when I didn't tell someone what I was thinking, he or she would keep repeating the annoying or hurtful behavior.

Surely, there's a better way. A good friend and I spend hours on the phone discussing such cases. We're quick to give each other advice: You don't have to have the last word. Realize that the other person may be dealing with his own issues. It's better to stop and reflect before telling him why you're angry or annoyed. If you feel the need to speak your mind, what is your end goal? What's the most effective way to get her to hear you? Will you ever change her? If not, how much of her behavior can you handle? How much of your emotional energy do you want to spend on this difficult relationship?

I could go on and on. And, on the phone, I'm afraid I do. But let's hear what these wise women have to say on the topic.

THE QUESTION

When you're feeling estranged or angry with someone, what have you learned about healing relationships? What have you learned about dealing with people you perceive to be difficult?

Pamela

Life does not always just happen. Sometimes you have to intentionally do stuff, whether or not it's comfortable.

My mother could be judgmental. She was so prickly that when I was having babies, she'd say terrible things to me, like "You're not going to nurse this baby too, are you?" I'd just hang up and cry. Her problem was that if I nursed the baby, then she couldn't feed him. She didn't come to visit very often anyway. After Dad died she re-did her life and opened up a dress store. So she started a whole new career in her early fifties.

When we were living at the farm, I didn't communicate much with her. But when I came back to town, I decided, *I am going to try and make this relationship work. I'm not doing it for her. I'm doing it for me.* So I designated one day a month to go see her. Sometimes I'd leave there crying. We were just two totally different people. But I stuck with it, so I got to see my mother grow older. I think in the end she really did like me, but it was an on-purpose thing. I could have just said, "I'm not going to call her. She never says anything nice to me."

My sister and I were both at the end of our rope trying to deal with her. We were flummoxed about how to be daughters to this woman because she was strong-minded, and she wanted her way. She was still trying to fix us. We went to a counselor about three or four times.

The counselor helped us understand that Mom is who she is. "Whatever she does, whoever she is, whatever she did—it's who she is. She can't be somebody else than herself," the counselor said. "When she says prickly things, you have to be tough enough to not let it bother you." That helped. When I face difficult people, I go with that.

One thing the counselor said really stuck with me. She said, "You know those see-through plastic tops they put over cakes? Just pretend you've got one of those, big enough to fit over your whole body. And when those critical words come, they can go *boing! boing!* and bounce off the surface. They don't have to go into your heart." That was a big lesson for me, and it worked. I still got my feelings hurt, but it helped me get by a little bit better.

As for other people in your life, I think you have to decide whether you want that relationship or not. I had a friend that lived near me for many years, and she was a bit prickly. As she got older, she got more opinionated. I'm sure she's depressed and negative, but I decided that I wanted to stay her friend. I'd call her when *I* felt good enough to talk to her. And I would just deal with it when she called me. But I treasure that friendship because it's so long-term.

I'm just very clear that you have to take care of yourself or else you cannot take care of anybody else. It sounds really selfish, but it's not.

Jane

I'm not sure that I have really always done a good job. I avoid conflict more often than I try to deal with it. In my work in the church at the regional and national level, I make a point of maintaining a speaking relationship with people whose votes are very different than mine on issues, and I hope I can keep doing that. Right now, I don't spend much time in the company of people who come from a different place. I suppose I'm more of an avoider now than I used to be.

One national-level task force deliberately put me with others who had different views. Our process emphasized the need to be open and in voice contact with people who view things differently. We didn't always talk about the issues on which we disagreed. It's very healing, I found, to make contact on the issues that you agree about. If the church is going to stay together in any form, it means that people have got to be willing to be with others who disagree. We don't have to get up and leave because of that. We can stay because we both see ourselves as members of a church that worships the triune God. I got to know some people who are adamantly against gays being ordained and against same-sex marriage, and I found that some of them are kind, gentle, good people.

Serving on that task force, I realized how important it is to me to have those personal relationships. I can remember particularly one pastor from Florida whose congregation is very conservative and he is, too. We had some exchange about a church that we had both been in. We found something in common that we could talk about. We kept up that relationship, even though he wouldn't feel at home at my church, and I wouldn't feel at home in his.

I hope that isn't glossing over something because we need to acknowledge our differences at the same time. I am convinced that we need each other, and I'm hoping that people of different viewpoints can stay together worshipping. Part of that is knowing each other as human beings, finding personal points of commonalities and beliefs and focusing on those without glossing over the actual differences.

Isabelle

My grandson's mother lived in New Orleans and is very southern. She was here once, and I had a discussion with her about health care. She got mad and stormed out. My daughter said to me, "Mother, you're very judgmental. Don't be judgmental." The next time, I kept it inside.

How do I deal with difficult people? I'm not very good at that. Sometimes I don't say anything and put on my happy face. Mostly I just avoid people who are difficult. Of course, if they're relatives, you can't.

When I have to see them, I stay away from difficult topics. I have to, because I have a tendency to explode about things that are near and dear to me. At my reunion, the women were talking about gay marriage. Most of my friends were saying, "Of course, they should be able to get married." But one friend said, "No. It's against the law." I looked at her and said, "Who made the law?" She said, "I don't know. It's the law." I said something like "That's not very caring." Another friend said, "Isabelle, she does care. She's a caring person."

I do things like that. I say things that I can't take back. That's how I deal with difficult people—I say the wrong things.

Joy

I have had trouble learning how to deal with difficult people. I've known two women who wanted to be in my life more than I wanted. They were manipulators who had their agenda, and they were used to getting their way. My problem was I was a "nice" person who wanted to please. In both cases, I spent some months torn up about how I was going to handle this because I could see that it was going to mean the breakup of friendship. In fact, it wasn't friendship; it was a power relationship with, in both cases, them wanting to be in control.

I just had to break it off. It made me miserable. You can't please everyone. There are people who need to control, and the only way to please them is to let them do what they want to do all the time.

That isn't the way I wanted to live. So I had to get some backbone. It was not easy for me.

Could I get entangled like that again? I don't think so. I think I learned how to spot controlling people. Not to get so close that you can't extract yourself.

Susan

The Bible says, "Love your neighbor as yourself." I always used to think that was a very egotistical thing, really bad, to love yourself. But I've learned that it's not good if you don't believe in yourself, if you don't realize that even with your foibles and shortcomings, you are a valuable person in your own right. Once you believe that, then you can love your neighbor. But if you don't like yourself, you don't like anybody else either. Finally, somebody made me realize that you have to believe in yourself. I can't do what you can do, and I can't do what my husband can do, and I can't do what my neighbor can do, but I can do what I can do. I am a valuable person, and I have something to contribute to the world.

It's not a matter of loving yourself too much. It's accepting and caring about yourself and taking care of your body, taking care of your mind, taking care of what you need.

Here is a little vignette about someone I met here at the retirement community. A couple of times, in two separate situations, I have found him in pieces psychologically. The first time, I was able to say to him, "Look, what you're going through is grieving. You are grieving the loss of your home, the loss of a familiar place." He said, "I never realized that."

The next time he was in pieces, he said, "I don't know how much longer I can go on." I said, "Look, what you need to do during this next week is feed your soul. You don't need to take care of your grandchildren. You don't need to do a bunch of yard work. What you need to do is go and read some good books. Feed yourself so that you have something to give to others. You've been giving out too much." Nobody had ever told him that. I gave him the name of a spiritual director and said, "It will take some time and effort, but you've got to find that for yourself." I could be his friend and understand where he was coming from, and I could also be supportive of him.

Some people are difficult. I will go my 50 percent of the way, but I'm not going to spend time trying to repair a relationship that is not going to be productive. Most of the people that I can't get along with are people who are in a totally different place—psychosocially, theologically, spiritually—from where I am. There's one person that I cannot understand. I will drop her a note or I will say, "Hi" and ask her how she is, but as far as being a close friend—I could never do that. I don't spend time working on relationships that are not going to be productive for both of us. You only have so much time. If it's not going to be a satisfying relationship for both parties, I have never been afraid to say something.

Katherine

I have a lifelong pattern. If things are tough emotionally, I figure that I'm responsible. My first thought is *What did I do?* And if I don't think I did anything wrong, I go into anger pretty fast. Neither of these tactics is successful, but I know that that's what I do.

My pattern is to go off by myself and try to figure this whole thing out. That's not always helpful either, because then I come back and I present a very well-thought-out rationale or defense—leaving no room for the other person.

I'm a beginner at this: In the moment, being able to say, "Could you tell me what's going on that's making you feel the way that you are feeling?" And then trying to listen, just so I can understand. To present my question as a matter of curiosity, rather than judgment. Rather than saying, "Why on earth would you think that?" I'm just not very good at it, yet.

Right now, I am reading a book called *Solving Tough Problems* by a former consultant. He worked with Shell Oil in South America trying to resolve some of the most difficult, conflicted issues on the planet. He writes that most of us are pretty good communicators; most of us can acquire the skills, if we haven't already, of presenting a very cogent, compelling argument. But we are lousy listeners.

I would say that that's still a learning piece for me. Even with my wife, Marie, and me. We can be very volatile and disengage, and I don't know whether I'm ever going to get back to the subject of our disagreement. That's not a good strategy. It's better to try to stay calm and be in a mode of curiosity about what's going on. Try to stay curious.

There's inquiry and there's advocacy. In consulting, they say you should make sure that you balance those. If there's a difficulty, you should do more inquiry, if you can do it honestly. Try to avoid advocacy dressed in sheep's clothing. That's a challenge for me. It's a growing edge.

It's easier to do it in consulting than in personal life. When I'm consulting, I can ask the right kind of questions and get them to hear. In personal life, it goes right out the window.

Anna

Conflict was such a controlling thing in my life. As a child, and for a long time afterwards, I didn't do anything that would create any conflict—in my marriage or any other relationships. I have had a couple of difficult relationships at work, and I did my best to speak to that person, to speak to the issue. I have a hard time—I still do—saying completely what's going on for me, even in my family. But it's far better than it used to be.

To me, conflict was something to avoid; it wasn't safe. I know I'm not alone; I've run into a lot of people like that.

I grew up with the belief that as long as everybody's happy, you're loved. "Take care of Mother. Take care of your brother. Don't bother your daddy." That was the underlying message. Creating conflict was a way not to be loved. Saying no really amounted to challenging what somebody had said or done. I've learned to say no, but it takes a toll on me still. It's not an easy thing to do, and I have to be deliberate. But I do it now, instead of completely avoiding all conflict. When it is important in a relationship with someone, I do it. But if it's not important, I don't do it.

To address the conflict, you speak to the person. You say, "I need you to know that I felt this way when you did such-and-such." In my family of origin, the other person would blow up. That's the risk, you see. You still are going to have to deal with their reaction, whether you want to or not. No matter how much you tiptoe.

Tiptoeing is not a good thing. It's better to be straightforward.

MY TAKEAWAYS

It's reassuring to hear that even wise folks sometimes have a hard time dealing with people. Isabelle admits that she says the wrong things. Katherine says she blames herself and then gets angry. Jane calls herself an avoider. Anna, after years of therapy, still has a hard time speaking to the issue when there is conflict.

It's also reassuring to hear that if it's not a close tie, you may have to just end the relationship as Joy did with two women friends. Susan advises not to spend time working on a relationship that is not going to be productive. Sometimes it's not worth the emotional energy. Pamela keeps up with one prickly friend, but only when she feels good enough to talk to her. She no longer makes blanket offers to help.

But when it's a close relative, you may feel compelled to maintain the relationship, even if the person is prickly, judgmental, critical, or controlling. The closer the relative, the more history you have, so old hurts quickly leap into each conversation. Those who know you best know exactly which buttons to press. It takes courage to be intentional, to choose to keep in touch when the other person keeps setting off your alarm bells.

Pamela's plastic cake cover sticks in my mind: When others criticize you, let the words go *boing! boing!* and bounce off. That's a useful mental tool. You need find a way to protect yourself when you interact with a difficult person. If you can't get the person out of your mind, then he's controlling you, even when you're not speaking.

Jane learned, by serving on a committee with people she totally disagreed with, how to maintain a speaking relationship with people who have opposing viewpoints. It's so tempting to take them by their collars and shake them till they hear reason and agree with you! Finding points of commonality makes sense, but what do you really gain by talking about the weather? I learned from Jane that creating and maintaining relationships with people you disagree with can help you to view them as human beings who see the world in a different way—instead of demonizing them. At least you understand, a little, why they feel that way.

Compassion is part of the answer. Some people have what I call a "social disability"— they just can't seem to get along with people. Their lives are littered with broken relationships. They don't know how to make it better. Yet perhaps they feel an even greater need for connection.

Understanding is step one. But you still have to learn how to interact. Katherine suggests staying calm and putting yourself in a mode of curiosity—truly trying to understand why the person is acting like a—well, like a person who sees the world in a different way. It helps to practice saying what Anna says they teach in therapy: "I need you to know how I felt when you . . ."

Maybe, if I practice these tactics enough, as in potty training, they will one day come naturally. If I do them consciously at first, I can hope that they will become habits of speaking, something I do unconsciously.

Or else I can keep saying the wrong things. Then nothing will get better.

Chapter 12

Managing Anger

I'VE READ THAT people express anger in one of two ways: they blow up or freeze up. I'm a freezer. When I'm super angry, I go silent. The screamers in my life don't necessarily notice. But my daughter grew up reading my moods, and once when she saw my lips tighten into that familiar thin line, she said, "Stop yelling at me!"

Only in recent years have I learned that freezing up can be as destructive as blowing up. Avoidance doesn't address the underlying problem or help solve it.

The experts say there is a third way to resolve disputes. Once the first wave of heat has passed, you get together and discuss your differences calmly, find out how both parties feel, and work toward a mutually acceptable solution. Obviously, that's easier said than done. I admire people who have devoted their lives to teaching dispute resolution skills at the personal level and the diplomatic level. I do believe that only when we learn to resolve personal disputes peacefully can we as a larger society figure out how to bring about peace globally.

In the meantime, what do you do when you're really, really mad? My husband believes you need to show your anger sometimes in order to get things done. If people feel threatened, they'll fall in line. But I've observed that once the shouting starts, it escalates, and the main result is hurt feelings. Each blowup provides fodder for the next one. In anger, people often say things they don't mean, exaggerating for effect, and the other person takes that to heart.

I admit—I'm a harmony freak. Family harmony, especially, is important to me. When my relatives blow up in anger at each other, I quake. I've observed that just one angry person can wreck family harmony. And when it's shattered, it takes a long time to rebuild.

So what is a better way to deal with anger?

THE QUESTION

Over the years, what have you learned about how to deal with or express your anger?

Joy

I admit I haven't always had self-control. As a mother, I was generally able to control my temper with little children, but one day I had a spectacular failure. When Elizabeth was sixteen, she begged to use the car on a day that the only car available was my husband's, and using his new car was not a good idea. Determined and impatient, and in spite of my quiet denial of permission, she went flying out to the garage, jumped in her father's car, and backed out so fast that she slammed his Volvo into the side of the door framework. Then she ran into the door itself because it had not finished going up! She damaged the doorframe, the garage door, and the car. I lost it! I had a total parental breakdown.

I heard someone shouting out of control, and it was me! Elizabeth was horrified of course at what she had done, and that was enough, really. I was appalled at myself. Later, I apologized, and she did too. We both learned a great deal about anger that day.

Anger is a lack of control. In the situation with Elizabeth, I should have stuck to the facts by saying, "You did a stupid thing. How are you going to explain this to your father?" And maybe,

"How are you going to pay for this?"

Nelson Mandela is my hero. Despite years in prison, after his release he forgave his captors. He simply did not waste his energy on anger. When I went to Africa, I saw the cell he was in; I saw the caves they made him work in and what they made him endure. I do not know how he did it. He came out of that experience such an admirable and loving spokesperson for all of humanity. It is no wonder that he was loved back.

Eva

Anger is something I deal with regularly. We need outlets for our anger, and I find that physical exercise helps. The YMCA has been my saving grace, my "other church."

Children need to have a way to express their anger, for sure. When our boys were little, we had a weighted inflatable clown that they were supposed to punch instead of taking it out on each other. They would slug old Bozo, and he'd bounce right back for more.

Being able to express anger verbally, without yelling, is helpful. Our younger son pointed that out to me when he was just a tot. There were times when I'd be at my wit's end over something that the boys had done. I wished that their father would deal with it but knew he wouldn't, so I'd be doubly angry and resort to yelling. I remember the little guy calmly saying to me, "Mom, it wouldn't be so bad if you just wouldn't yell."

I thought, *You know, he's right.*

Jane

I probably don't have good ways of dealing with anger because I tend to deny it in the first place. I really haven't thought about that. What makes me angry?

Sometimes when I get angry, I tell people. Sometimes I bottle it up, but I do think I deny that I'm angry. Maybe it comes out in other ways; for instance, I remind people of things they've done. Ideally, I would like to be able to say, "I really didn't like what you did. What can we do about that?" I'm not a shouter, but I'm trying to speak up when I'm angry about things.

Anna

The biggest help from therapy was that I tapped into all the unexpressed anger about all the times that I didn't get to say no in my childhood and adulthood. My therapist was good at helping me express it. In a safe setting with my therapist, I would get spitting, off-the-wall mad.

Before, I didn't pay any attention to my anger. It was buried. There was so much of it that I couldn't handle it. When something new came up and it required a no, it was very scary to learn how to say it. It took a lot of effort, but I have gradually learned to do that.

That's the issue: helping yourself say no when you need to and recognizing when you can't do anything about it.

So what are you going to do with your anger? If I get really angry, and I don't want to express it at the person, or if the situation can't be changed, I need to find some way to cope with my anger. How? Well, I haven't had reason to do this lately, but for a while I had an old badminton racquet, and I would pound the heck out of a pillow. I would do this at home, by myself, when no one was around. It only takes five minutes to beat the heck out of it. You have to shout at the same time, "No, I don't want to!" over and over, for about five minutes. You would be surprised what you can unload. That was a skill I learned from my therapist. Of course, you want to do something that is not going to hurt you. Don't put your fist through the wall!

Sometimes you speak to the person and sometimes you don't. That depends on the situation. There are times when I wouldn't ever do that and other times when it's absolutely called for. You need to say, "I want you to know this is not okay."

I also learned to use "I" language: I feel, I think, I believe, I want, I need. That's how I counsel couples who are going to get married: learn to express the "I" language in an argument. Talk about yourself, where you're coming from. Instead of saying, "You need to stop doing that," say, "I want you to stop doing that, because when you do that I feel you are discounting me." Instead of saying, "You don't believe what I've said," say, "What I want is for you to do such-and-such, and if it doesn't happen, tell me why you're not doing that; I need to know that." "You" language tends to back somebody in the corner, because it is finger-pointing. That's a way to make people defensive, and they're not going to do what you want.

Now always remembering to use "I" language first—that's the hard part.

Ruth

Anger is not an easy thing for me. I don't do anger well at all. I just clam up. I am convinced that that's not good for me. I wish I could be more open. My parent's marriage was long and loving—they adored each other. But they didn't model for my sister and me how to express our anger.

I can remember one time in my kids' lives when I *did* let it all out. (Something tells me they could remember more.) All four of us were on the way to Bible school. They were squabbling with each other in the backseat. I stopped the car and screamed bloody murder at them. Of course it had to be on the way to Bible school! They were just driving me batty. And there I was, a church-lady mom, just losing it! Such an irony. What you say in anger, you cannot take back.

In my new marriage, I am working on this. Maybe I express my anger with Paul more than I need to, simply because he's so accepting and open. He is just unbelievably good-natured. But when he finally becomes annoyed or angry, he says it in a way that you get it. But then his anger is gone. Fifteen minutes later, he's back to normal. That's good. I'm not like that, and I do admire him.

Katherine

Anger is a challenge; maybe because I'm the child of an angry mother.

What I've learned about anger is this: anger may be a manifestation of depression. My sister and I have talked about this; maybe that was my mother's problem. My mother had a sister who was the depressive of the family, who had electroshock therapy treatments periodically when we were growing up. That aunt was always just lovely and sweet, if a little bit vague because she had come out of the hospital. It was my mother who was the volatile one, as far as I could tell. Mother had never had half a Prozac in her life, but I think some of her anger may have been depression that got turned outward. When I blow up and find myself being very angry, it's troubling to me because I don't know if it's genuine anger or just this genetic tendency.

My anger can be very wounding because if I really explode I can kick somebody out of the car or slam the door, and I don't like that. I haven't befriended the angry part of me. The Queen of Hearts is the way I referred to my mother. It occurred to me the other day that maybe I have that Queen of Hearts in me. I try to keep it under wraps.

When I'm really angry at somebody, I feel like I'm out of control. I'm pretty good with words, and I can just lash out with words. If we are going to have an argument, I can stick right with it. If I feel like I can't any longer, I will just leave. It's not healthy.

To deal with it, I try to disengage. I say, "I'm just not able to talk about this right now. Can we talk about this tomorrow?" That is a whole lot better than turning on my heels and walking away, or being walked away from.

I've learned that it's not always something I've done. I tell myself, *Don't be so self-centered that you think everything is your responsibility. Take care of yourself, if you can. Hold it a little bit more lightly.*

Introverts go inside and figure it all out. By the time they come outside, they have it so perfectly polished and phrased that there isn't any room for anybody else to tinker with it. What we have to do instead is say, "Here's a topic. When can we talk about it?" It's important for me to get back to the topic with the other person before I completely bake the whole situation in my own head. Then we can have a two-way decision. Otherwise one of us has already made the decision and there's no room for the other one to get in there and play with it.

Susan

Anger takes an incredible amount of your emotional energy. The older I get, the more I try very hard to think, *Do I have the emotional energy to be angry about this?* There are situations that I look at and say, *No, I'm not going to get angry about that. I don't have any spare energy to spend on that.* That's part of being able to draw back, emotionally. I tend to impulsively say, "I'm angry about this!" Now I remind myself to count to ten before saying something. That gives me perspective.

Believe me, I say this is an *ideal* state, because we all fail. I can't say that every time I get myself into a state, I've thought about it, and I've decided I'm going to be angry or I'm not going to be angry. But that's the ideal.

What do they say? "It takes many more muscles to frown than it does to smile." Whether that's true or not, I don't know, but it's a good thought.

In a meeting if things are going badly, I will get quiet. If I have to talk, I will talk very quietly and very slowly, because I find that that calms things down and focuses things. If you start talking loudly, then everybody else starts talking loudly. Then it gets worse.

It's very rare that I get angry with friends or acquaintances. If my husband says something to me that I think is demeaning, I will immediately flare. He doesn't mean to do that, ever, because he's just not that kind of person. But if I take it wrong, then I say something and then it's over. Never, never, do I harbor a grudge. I will say what I think, get it out on the table, and then it's over. That is much easier for me, emotionally, to just get all the pieces on the table. I say, "I'm willing to listen, but this is the way I feel."

It's hard because people say things one way, and I hear them from my point of view when in all probability they're coming from their point of view and the two are very different. We often imbue other people with our frame of reference. That's stupid, but we all do it. We think that everybody is coming from where we're coming from, which is not the case. Or they don't mean it. It's good to say, "I heard you say x. Is that what you mean?" Even that much helps the situation. Sometimes they didn't really mean that.

I don't know if you've ever had the experience of seeing somebody, a friend, and you say, "Hi," and they say, "Hi" and just keep on walking. You think, *What have I done wrong?* Something is bothering that person. Nine times out of ten they've had a fight, or they've had some bad news, or they feel sick, whatever. It's not you. So continue to respond, and the next time you see them say, "Hi, how are you?" And that person will probably say, "Gee, it's good to see you. I haven't seen you for so long."

Change and conflict are givens. It's not a question of if you're going to accept it; it's how you go about dealing with the conflict. Instead of saying, "It's got to be my way," it's better to say, "I'm here to listen." I think that we need to understand that.

You can't avoid conflict. You get two people in a room and you've got five opinions about something. The more you try to avoid conflict, the worse it becomes. It takes on a much greater importance than if you look at it and say, "This is what's going on," lay the cards on the table, and see what kind of a hand you have. That's better than keeping the cards all face down and saying, "I don't have to play this hand." You have to play them all. Instead of avoiding conflict, see what matters to the other person, figure out how you can come to an agreement, or agree to disagree.

My dad was a salesman, but in his later years he became a troubleshooter for the Bureau of Labor and Industry, for the state. He traveled all over, talking to workers who were angry beyond words with what their employers or the government had done to them.

My dad was a big man, six foot one, just a big, happy guy. He said, "I can't tell you how many times I've been met with a shotgun at the door." My dad's first words were always, "I came to hear what's going on." Then he would get a volley of angry words. Then he'd say, "Now tell me the rest of the story," and another volley. A third time, he'd say, "Now, have you left any details out? Is there anything else that we can talk about that will help me understand what's going on?" Then he'd begin to try to sift through all the facts and find out what was going on. By the time he was done, the angry man would be offering him a beer.

Dad's motto was "Never leave a person until you can make him laugh."

Isabelle

Sam never got mad at people. He would get mad at inanimate objects, like if he was fixing the computer. I would try to make it all right because I couldn't stand seeing him angry. Then if I got mad, I would tirade, and he would just stay quiet. It was maddening sometimes, but then I'd calm down and we'd be fine.

He never would lose his temper with me. But sometimes he would do things, and I would really get angry. I'll give an example. I was in a terrible car accident and my friend was killed. I was going to Ashland with three friends, and my friend was driving. We got a $25,000 settlement from my friend's insurance company, and I thought, *Good, we'll use that to have fun*. But Sam took the money and invested it in the stock market. I'll never forget how angry I was. He knew how I felt, but it wouldn't change him. I finally forgave him and thought, *Well, that's the way it is*. All my screaming and yelling didn't work.

But sometimes it's good to explode and let it go; then it smoothes things out and it's okay. Sometimes you have to vent. Maybe that's why Sam had a bad heart; he never vented. The last time we were in Egypt, it was horrid for him. The work situation was terrible, because he was in charge, and he was having huge problems trying to deal with everyone back here, as well as some Egyptians who weren't being effective. He even got fired from the job, although not from the company, and someone else took over. I asked, "Doesn't that make you feel bad?" But he stayed calm and said, "Oh no, it was just an experience." He later wrote that he was angry about that, but he didn't vent. He kept his feelings inside, and he would drink because that was what numbed him. That worried me for a while. But that was just a temporary phase.

MY TAKEAWAYS

Many pearls of wisdom gleam amidst this flood of good suggestions. The idea of pounding a pillow with a badminton racquet reminded me of an idea I heard once: write down the things that are making me mad and then tear the paper into pieces and throw them away. I did that, and it helped.

Clearly, the two extremes don't work. Clamming up is bad for the body and soul. It can even lead to a bad heart or drinking. Isabelle says, "Sometimes you have to vent" because it "smoothes things out." I've heard others say this, too, but this is not my experience. Too often, mean words are spoken, and they cannot be taken back.

I liked hearing the perspective that sometimes you speak up and sometimes you don't. This makes sense to me. There are definitely occasions when speaking your mind won't make things better. You just have to deal with your anger and soldier on. But on other occasions, you really should let people know how you're feeling.

It depends a lot on the other person and how receptive he or she is to criticism at that moment. If the other person is feeling vulnerable and insecure, even "I feel" language can put her on the defensive. If you've known this person a long time and have tried many times to get him to change, it may be better to put your anger aside and choose to get along.

Also, it depends on how much emotional energy you have for

the particular issue. If it's not that important to your life, count to ten and drop it. Pick your battles, and engage only when it matters. If you're in a large group where others always have their weapons drawn, leave and find a community where you are more comfortable. Don't just stand there, waiting to be shot.

In the heat of the moment, sometimes it's better to disengage. If you know you're about to say wounding things, pull away until you feel calmer, then deal with the issue later. But don't try to resolve the whole thing yourself, offstage, assigning blame where it's due; come back and talk it over with the person.

Sometimes just speaking in a quieter, calmer voice will diffuse tensions. It helps to realize that other people may not be coming from the same place we are. Maybe they've just had a fight with someone or they feel sick.

I need to practice "I" language and "hands-on-the-table" conversation:

+ "I want you to stop doing that, because when you do that I feel . . ."

+ "I heard you say x. Is that what you mean?"

+ "I'm willing to listen, but this is the way I feel."

As Susan says, "Change and conflict are givens. The question is not how to avoid conflict, but how do you handle it."

Chapter 13

Emerging from Dark Places

SERIOUS MENTAL ILLNESSES, obviously, need professional treatment. However, many people suffer from depression or anxiety that is not crippling but occasionally pulls them into places of deep sadness or nervous fear. Whether or not they've ever been treated, they've had to find ways to identify when the problem is recurring and discover mindsets that will help get them through the next bout.

Others are luckier and don't suffer from either depression or anxiety, but they still struggle with negative thoughts, such as self-pity or a tendency to make harsh judgments about themselves or others. These "automatic negative thoughts" can be just as hard to dislodge once they get into your brain loop. If you're cynical or pessimistic, you're likely to create a self-fulfilling prophecy. If you think you can't do something, you won't. Once you start thinking negatively about someone, it's hard to feel compassionate toward that person.

The field of positive psychology fascinates me. I love the idea that psychology has moved from focusing solely on the treatment of mental illness to helping people develop a more upbeat frame of mind.

One popular book suggests we identify our evil twins as "gremlins," assign them names and personalities, and defang them. *Taming Your Gremlin: A Surprisingly Simple Method for Getting Out of Your Own*

Way, by Rick Carson, gives concrete suggestions for how to silence your inner critic and stop self-defeating behaviors.

Whichever is your negative thought of choice (or not choice!), there have to be better ways of dealing with it. Part of wisdom, surely, is the ability to develop methods for detecting the onset of negative thoughts and finding ways to minimize them, if not banish them.

THE QUESTION

When you're feeling negative—whether depressed, anxious, judgmental, or self-pitying— how do you get yourself out of it?

Pamela

When I'm in the pit, it's hard to make myself do anything. There are a variety of ways I try to pull myself out of it. I go back to books that have nurtured me in the past. I just keep doing it until my spirits lift.

One of the things I'm pretty good at is saying, *Okay, today I have to do such-and-such.* It makes me depressed to not want to do anything. But when I don't get anything done, it makes me *more* depressed! I'm not talking about big stuff, just taking care of the house. I try not to overwhelm myself with a list of fifty things to do, but pick one and just do it. Sometimes I just walk around the house and wonder what I should do next. I think, *Focus, just focus!* or *Just do it!* At the end of the day, I feel better even if all I did was one thing. Sometimes it's just getting dinner on the table. I've never gotten so low that I haven't gotten dinner on the table. I have the gumption to do it, but when I'm in the pit, I have to push myself.

In the process of coming out of that pit, I've been to group counseling. I have a group of friends that I meet with about once a month. We all suffer from depression, so we give each other strength.

I've known for years and years that I need to get out and walk.

I just don't like exercise, never have. I have gotten hooked up with a friend that I walk with three days a week. That is very helpful, to have to get up for something. Most of the time, I drag myself out of bed and think, *Oh, I wish I didn't have to do this.* But the tenacity I have is just to *push* and say, *Okay, this is what you're going to do.* On the other days, I do yoga. Sometimes I really just don't want to do anything. But if I've made arrangements and I've made a commitment, then I'll do it.

Katherine

I have to get physically moving. I try to go out and take a good long walk or hit some golf balls. It's great for writer's block, too. When I was consulting, if I had a tricky situation and I didn't know how to approach it, I just went for a walk, and nine times out of ten I'd come home with an idea.

Music helps, too. I used to play the piano a lot, especially if I was in a bad space. I took piano for years and years. Yesterday, I got out my old recital pieces and started to see if I could make my fingers come back. It's just balm. I love it.

If I'm really depressed, I can't move. I think, *It's raining. Why would I want to go out?* or *It's too much trouble to go over to the Y and get some exercise.* Yet that is exactly what I need. If I make myself do it, I'm in much better shape.

Sometimes I read, but reading is escape. I don't think reading in the middle of depression is really a big help, not as much as moving my body. If I'm depressed, I can sit and read a book for three days. It distracts me a little bit, but it doesn't lift me out of it.

A little antidepressant helps. As the saying goes, "Better living through chemistry!" I don't discount that. It's been a long time since I have had to use it. Interestingly enough, depression doesn't happen to me in the winter. It's nothing to do with a lack of sunshine. It comes to me in June. I don't know why. It feels like the clouds roll in, and I'm having to fight my way up to be present. I take half of this little pill, and the clouds lift.

Ruth

During those difficult years with my first husband, writing was very helpful to me—poetry and journal writing. I wrote a lot. That was probably one of the very best things for me to do. Both the poetry and the journal writing became a release—and, in a sense, a form of prayer. But then I think life is a form of prayer.

I did feel a lot of anger at the injustice of our not having been informed by anyone in Tom's family that he was at risk for Huntington's, which is a genetic disease. His father had died at Anzio during World War II when he was too young to have shown that he had the gene; his paternal grandmother was "put away" in an asylum. Each of our children has a 50 percent chance of having Huntington's disease. I've been reading old journals, and it's all there: the sadness, the anxiousness, the frustration for him and for me. Writing it all out was extremely helpful in climbing out of darkness. So was throwing myself into chopping down blackberry brambles and waxing our old, splintered pine floors. And Shakespeare's kind of sleep, sleep "that knits up the raveled sleeve of care."

Isabelle

I am judgmental inside my head. I go over it and over it, and I want to get rid of it. I just start reading something, usually something light. Or I like to watch movies on Netflix.

I try to understand why I'm being so judgmental about people. Why does that person have to be like me? That person does not have to be like me. Why do I think that my way is right and their way is wrong? That is a hard thing to figure out. They are just as right as I am. It might have something to do with feeling better about yourself if you can find something wrong about someone else. You think, *Oh, well at least I'm better than that.* It's a terrible thing to feel that way. It doesn't go anywhere.

If I can talk to my daughter Annie, it's all right. She'll tell me when I'm doing something unkind. Her husband is wonderful, and he'll tell me, too. For instance my Annie's very best friend since high school is an actress, and she's polyamorous. She has a group, and they're all married—so she's having sex a lot with different people. That was very hard for me to accept. Once, we were going to go to the theatre together. When she cancelled last minute, I found out she went to a hotel to have sex with someone. I was very angry.

My son-in-law takes me down a peg and tries to explain how things are with her and how we have to accept her the way she is—if we want to be her friend. He says, "Let's try to see her side of it. You know I have a lot of trouble with her, too. I've had to figure out how to live with the way she is."

Annie is very good, and she'll tell me when she thinks I'm way off track. When I see how she sees people, it helps me too. I don't know how she got that way, but she's great.

Joy

First of all, I do know that negativity does not resolve problems. So what did I do with the awful news of macular degeneration in my eyes? It was the "first trial" of accepting aging, for me. I had to realize that someday I would be blind—and Jeff's not here to help me. I admit I was scared of the unknown, of that grave diagnosis. A dear friend offered to take me to visit her artist friend Margaret, who was in the advanced stages of the disease. She was fully blind. My friend told me that Margaret would be inspirational. I couldn't understand how that could possibly be true. Margaret met us at the door of her retirement home. She explained that they had given her the first apartment in the hallway and that the residence had offered to hang her paintings throughout the hallway. She was full of gratitude to be able to "show" us her art as we walked together! Here indeed was a very happy (blind) artist. Back in her apartment, we talked a while about how she managed to continue to paint. She explained that she knows where the colors are on her palette, and now she has switched to abstract art! Later she offered us tea. She went to the stove and turned on the burner, where there was a teapot waiting. She had cups and saucers on the countertop and asked if one of us would pour the hot water when it boiled. "That is the only thing I cannot do," she said. She was such a gracious hostess that I appreciated and was amazed at all she did. Her attitude made us both feel like there was nothing lacking. Afterwards she took us on a walking tour of her facility. Indeed she was inspirational. Attitude is everything.

Susan

If I'm tempted to be judgmental, I try to look at the situation and say to myself, *No, I'm not going to put that person down. It's not as bad as I think.* It's true—some things are bad. But then I start looking at that person, seeing what can be done about him or her, and getting as broad a view as I can of whatever the situation is. I really try to be positive and thankful. That's one of the big things in my life, being thankful.

I have one friend who is negative, and she has every reason to be. But I'm not going to participate in her negativity. I try to do things for her, like take her out for lunch when it's her birthday. But I don't respond to her negative e-mails, and I don't respond to her negative thoughts. I try to make her laugh. I don't have the emotional energy to spend a lot of time with that kind of negativity.

As I've grown older, I know that my emotional energy bank is smaller than when I was young. So am I going to spend that deposit? Or am I going to leave that deposit there? Am I going to write a small check or a big check? I can't waste a whole lot of what I have. I have to make it count for something.

I'm pretty self-disciplined in many ways. I'm not going to spend a bunch of time with people that are negative. And I can't waste the time being negative myself. I'm not trying to put myself up as any paragon of virtue; I'm just like anybody else. All we can do is try.

Jane

Prayer has helped. I hesitate to say a different relationship with God, but I guess that's the best way to put it.

When I was younger, I was more judgmental and critical. Absolutely. I still recognize the tendency in myself. It's not that I've lost it, it's that I have a different understanding. This comes out of the gospels: the idea that we are all accepted. I look for God's gifts through other people that I might not have appreciated before. It's more of an openness.

I think I have found a way to deal with critical thoughts. It's not that I have intentionally done that. It's part of my spiritual life. I'm aware of them when they come up and I say, *Is there something I can do about this? Is there something I should be doing?*

Anna

I've learned that we have an ongoing commentary in our heads, sometimes more than one. I've got a worrier in there who frets and stews about things that aren't done and who will, especially while lying down and going to sleep, remember mistakes and things we wish we hadn't done. I say, *Stop! We aren't going to go there.* It's a "we" thing because I actually had a dissociative disorder. That's why my memory of abuse was hidden and had to be recalled.

I have more than one voice in my head, which is true for most of us. One of them is a child who whines that everything is too hard. Another one is in charge. She wants to run everything and requires it to be perfect with no mistakes, and she has to get everything done. She carries the guilt; that is the main issue for her. I have got these voices inside me, but they're no longer in control all the time. Once in a while they surface, and I then have to say, *Wait. Stop.*

The healing was bringing all of these back together into one person. That's why it took so much therapy, because every memory of abuse had a different identity, so to speak. Everybody's got more than one voice inside. You've got the nag. You've got the kid that wants to play. I acknowledge that they're different parts of me.

We're one because I'm in charge now, as the adult, which is what "my children" need. They're safer when there is an adult in charge, who's going to keep them safe. But you know how hard it is to say no to children.

I've been on antidepressants for years and will continue, maybe for the rest of my life. I have what's called dysthymia, which is low-grade chronic depression. I tried doing without the medication, and it doesn't work. Now that things are tough with my husband's health at home, I've had to ramp it up a little bit. I had a couple of meltdowns, and that tells me that I'm not caring for me as well as I need to—for two reasons: for me and so I can do a better job caring for him.

I had an outstanding therapist. His ability to be with you, where you are right now and not somewhere else is amazing. My time with him was the most wonderful gift.

Eva

My "drug of choice" is exercise. When I sensed I was headed for a depression, I was determined not to take antidepressants. I know they help some people, but my elderly mother suffered a terrible depression, and I think antidepressants compounded her problem. Exercise has proven to be good medicine in my case.

Also church. Faith. Faithful friends. Family. Professional counseling. They've all helped me through dark places. And music. When I learned that my husband had another woman in his life, it occurred to me that I could never listen to another love song. I felt that crummy. Then something amazing happened. One weekend, my radio was tuned to a station that was playing nothing but love songs. As I listened to them, I heard every one of them as a hymn. Each love song was to God or from God, about me loving God and God loving me. Now I can listen to love songs knowing that God loves me.

Talking to my pastor helped immeasurably too. I told him, "I know God loves me, but I have a longing to have someone in my life to share a physical love, too. Is that wrong?" He assured me that it wasn't, that it was perfectly understandable.

After a while a wonderful gentleman came into my life. He nourished me lovingly—spiritually and physically—and gave me a sense of worthiness. My kids loved him too. It was a very lovely love. Our years together were full of fun, good conversation, mutual admiration, and travel. As we grew closer, a thought about love, one that Swedish thinker and peacemaker Ellen Key expressed years ago, resonated with me. She said that love without legal marriage may be moral, but legal marriage without love is never moral. I checked that out with my pastor and he concurred.

My love and I talked seriously of marrying, but it was not to be. Sadly, he was diagnosed with a particularly aggressive disorder. Even so, our last months together were full of joy. This man knew how to make the most of life. He was never morose. He appreciated it all. He tackled illness as an opportunity to gain more education. He studied medical books and amassed a collection of texts that would be the envy of many doctors, I'm sure. Even though he has passed on—it's been eight years now—he is still a comforting, strengthening part of my life.

MY TAKEAWAYS

A very lovely love, a wonderful gentleman, a sense of worthiness. Don't you love it?

We can't count on such a person swooping into our life and making us feel better. But each of the women had some very concrete suggestions. Some may work for you and some may not, but the list is worth reviewing:

+ Exercise: a long walk, yoga, golf, a trip to the gym.

+ Sing or play music.

+ Go to therapy or counseling.

+ Consider taking antidepressants: they are not for everybody, but sometimes after half a pill, the clouds lift.

+ Write: poetry or journal entries.

+ Distract: reading or movies.

+ Take a long talk with someone you trust.

+ Consider: how bad could it get? Others have had it much worse.

+ Figure out what can be done, and do it.

+ Take as broad a view as possible.

+ Be thankful for the good things.

+ Tell the negative thoughts, *Stop! No!* and try to let the adult inside you take control.

+ Find a community full of positive people.

Chapter 14

Recovering from Failure

I KNOW SOMETHING OF failure, although I admit it's not my favorite subject.

My husband advised me not to quit my good job with a respected national magazine to write a novel. I was the West Coast business and technology correspondent, and the magazine sent me to Silicon Valley to interview some of the giants of the tech world, including Steve Jobs, Scott McNealy, and Gordon Moore. But I had tasted the sweetness of book writing, and I had a terrific idea for a novel about Marco Polo and his secret love.

Seven years later, I had completed a manuscript of six hundred pages, my "magnum opus." I had sought and absorbed feedback on every chapter from my writing instructor and a critique-group class, several times over. My agent presented it to the best historical fiction editors in the country. They all said no. Of course, rejection is part of the process of submitting to publishers. But by August that year, there were no more options.

Total failure.

You're supposed to learn from failure, right?

After thrashing about in the gloom, I realized I did have some options. I could put my novel in the bottom drawer and forget about it. I could self-publish it. Or I could do as my agent had suggested and rewrite it as a young adult novel. Although the young-adult book category was hopping, I resisted this idea; I had not written my magnum opus for teenagers.

Still, this last idea was the best of my three options, so I decided to give it a try. I cut my novel in half and streamlined the plot. The following June, my agent submitted it to several young-adult fiction editors, and he sold it to Random House in less than a week.

Of course, the full story is more complicated, but that is the gist of it. I did learn something from that failure: the importance of being adaptable and of trying different avenues. Could I do it again? Not sure. It takes a lot out of you.

THE QUESTION

How do you bounce back from setbacks or failures?

Katherine

I have not been a huge risk taker in my life. I think that I've walked a safe line so that I wouldn't have huge failures. I live with someone who is an enormous risk taker. So I compare myself to her. I'm always the one who's saying, "What if? What if?" I can conjure up terrible scenarios and begin to adjust so they won't come to pass.

When I'm in a failure situation, I go into a deep period of self-examination, because I'm always pretty sure it was my fault. It's hard to admit when I have contributed to some failures. I'm thinking of a consulting job I had once, and it went to hell in a handcart. Looking back, I know that there were some decisions I made that contributed to it. Once I realized that, I contacted the client. He was a former client at that point and likely to remain so. But I did want to get together with him and process it a little bit and say, "I realize I did this and this, and I wanted to tell you I'm sorry." He just said, "Oh, that was then. This is now. That was nothing!" I know he didn't feel that way when it happened, because I felt the sting at the time when he lashed out. Nonetheless, he couldn't have that conversation. Maybe he wasn't ready.

When things go wrong, I usually retreat, beat myself up, and then go through a big period of time thinking about what I could have done differently. And then I address it if I can, or say, *That's enough of that. Let's move on.*

Susan

Unfortunately, sometimes we don't teach our children to fail. We teach them how to win or be gracious winners, but you have to learn to be a gracious loser, too. In the Olympics, if you don't win a gold medal, silver isn't bad. It's the same way in life. Losing isn't the end of your world.

When facing setbacks, you just keep putting one foot in front of the other, continually. My husband says he was never the head of the class but was a good solid middle. By putting one foot in front of the other, he arrived. I really think that's part of what life is all about. If you let your setbacks destroy you because you're afraid you're going to fail, then you've made the choice to be a failure.

It's not easy to go back and say, *Okay, I'll keep going.* It can be painful.

When I think of failures or setbacks, I think of my experience raising kids. Our son Peter, particularly, just completely shut us out of his life and made choices that didn't work out well for him. But we always said, "We love you. We're here." And in the end, the only place he wanted to be was with us.

It's not because we understood his life. We accepted him even though he lived an alternative lifestyle. He was a very contrary person, but he wanted to be with us at the end. I'll never forget one moment when he was at hospice: He was sedated pretty heavily so that he could be comfortable. I leaned over to him, and I could see that he was still there. I said, "Peter, we love you." He said, "Why are you telling me that now?" I said, "Because I want you to always remember that." He said, "Well, that goes without saying."

Setbacks and successes can be cyclical. Another one of our sons made some choices that we didn't agree with, but we supported him and said, "If this is how you feel, have you thought about so-and-so?" We said it once and left it. Then we were there when things went the way we thought they were going to go. It's not that we were wiser, it's just that we had a longer vision than he did. You can't beat somebody up for not having longer vision when they're less than half your age! But we were there. He got through that setback, and now he's happy.

How do you climb out of bad stuff? I guess it's the choice to climb out. Sometimes it is very hard to even lift that first foot and say, *Okay, I will take a step forward. I will do this. Every bone in my body says no way. But I will go forward.*

Isabelle

Oh, failure! I failed a lot. If you don't feel like you're doing a good job, it feels like failure. That's happened to me.

One particular thing happened at a local theater, and it's still inside me and it boils up occasionally. I was acting in a role that I loved. I don't know if I was a failure or if the director just thought I was. I didn't do what he was hoping. All actors get notes. He'd bring me notes before the performance, and I'd get all confused. It was hard.

After the last performance, on a Saturday night, the cast and crew always stayed to help clean up. I was there till one o'clock in the morning, and the director never came and said thank you. When I left, nobody said good-bye. That stuck in my craw and stayed there. That makes me think I was a failure. He never asked me to do anything again. I sent in my resume for other plays, and they didn't even answer.

It was horrible. I'm still dealing with it. That was the worst. Failures are little and big, and there are some you don't remember. I let this one build up.

What did I learn? I feel that I should have worked harder, that

I didn't do my homework. I didn't do a lot of stage work after that. Well, I did act at one other theater, and I enjoyed it a lot. One summer, I auditioned for four roles and I didn't get any of them, so I gave up. By then, my husband wasn't doing well, so it was probably for the best that I stayed home. Sometimes you just give up on something and that's the way it is.

But I still did commercial work. I got to do a movie about Alzheimer's, and that was more acting, and I felt good about it. I was given a copy of that video on disc, and I could watch myself. I thought, *Hey, that's not too bad.* That was a wonderful experience.

Joy

This is a story of disappointment and struggle.

In 1986, I'd been on the national women's advocacy committee for three years, and two of us were eligible for reelection. Because my first election had been so straightforward, I was not at all concerned. I asked my husband to come to this national meeting because I wanted him to experience the positive energy I felt from the whole church as it worked through many difficult issues of the day. Little did I know that I was to be the focus of a personal challenge.

My husband and I walked into the enormous arena with all the bright lights and electronic reader boards above us. The nominating committee came to the podium and announced that the advocacy team on issues concerning women would be the first committee to be presented. They were going in alphabetical order. They announced, "We have two people up for reelection, and we have two challengers." My challenger was a pastor, and I was a layperson. She was young, and I was a bit older. She had been involved with prison ministry. I thought, *I'm a dead duck.* The only things going for me were that I had been chair of the committee and had experience, and the nominating committee had approved my reelection. But was that enough? I had a sense that this was an ideological challenge to our committee. We'd been pushing for progress on gay and lesbian issues in the church and also to protect a woman's right to choose abortion.

When they called for the vote, Jeff was sitting next to me, watching this democratic Presbyterian system that I'd been raving about to him. The vote was 51 percent to 49 percent. I *barely* won—by a whisker! The whole auditorium went "oooh!" People were in shock that the vote was so close.

Then my friend Roberta's name came up. She's young and dynamic, in line to be next year's chair, but her challenger was also a young woman pastor with good credentials. Still, it seemed obvious that this was a radical effort to change the direction of our work. The challenger won—52 percent to 48 percent. The only thing we could figure out was that the church voters were thinking, *Let's give one to the committee and one to the challengers.* It was happenstance that my last name came first, alphabetically. If my name had come second, Roberta would probably have won and I would have lost.

The vote reflected the dynamics of the church, which was becoming very divided on sensitive issues. The conservative delegates were starting to use computers to contact their supporters. This was the beginning of negative politicking of hot issues in the church, issues that became very nasty in later months and years.

Our committee had a little room where we ate lunch, and we always opened it up to anybody who wanted to come. It happened that the room next door had a mike for their lunch gathering, and one of the far right groups was meeting there. We could hear someone shout, "Let's have a cheer for getting Roberta off the women's committee!" They cheered. We were devastated. That's when we knew we were under attack.

I had to face the grave disappointment that my "wonderful" church was extremely divided by politics. One group of people was working hard to achieve their ends, which were the opposite of our goal of responding to women's concerns. I didn't question their right to nominate candidates who supported their positions, but I was saddened by their stealth attack and their glee in defeating my colleague. The woman that they elected to our committee tried to undo many of the changes we had begun, and that felt to me like a setback for all women in the church. After she joined, the press that supported her point of view monitored our meetings, and their reports seemed provocative and aimed at stirring up discord. My last three years on the committee were much more difficult than the first three. We struggled to be open to the minority view even when it opposed our committee's raison d'être.

So how did it affect my faith? Really strongly. Because of this ugliness in the very heart of the church, I understood a lot more about Jesus. I began to appreciate what a radical he was speaking out for those who had no voice, and how when he spoke for the disenfranchised, his message upset not only the Pharisees but the rulers. As we know, they plotted how to get rid of him, even wanting to kill him. I'd never truly felt that before, at a gut level. Now I have.

After that, I made a practice of sitting with the opposition during worship. They were not particularly happy when I came over, but I did it because I wanted to reach out, to be available to talk to them. For the most part, they didn't talk to me, but at least I tried. Later, other women took up the work I started, and eventually the church became more flexible.

MY TAKEAWAYS

In Silicon Valley, "embrace failure" is a buzzword. Investors encourage young entrepreneurs to jump in quickly and start up new companies; if the company fails, the entrepreneur is lauded as someone who is willing to take risks. Every time an entrepreneur's startup fails, she looks more attractive the next time around, because she is experienced and knows what mistakes not to repeat. "Failure" is seen as a synonym for "learning experience." Silicon Valley even has an annual event called FailCon that celebrates and studies startup failures. It's considered better to take a risk and fail than to stay in your comfort zone and refuse to act on your dream.

But when it's *your* failure, in *your* life, it's hard to see it in any positive light.

Still, the way I look at it, you can react to failure in one of two ways: You can let it crush you, or you can figure out how to learn from it.

What do these stories teach us about recovering from setbacks? If you let your setbacks destroy you, then you've made the choice to be a failure. So don't let them destroy you. Keep putting one foot in front of the other. Choose to climb out. Find ways to bounce back.

Chapter 15

Rethinking Aging

IN OUR FORTIES and fifties, most of us don't want to think about aging. The topic makes us squirm. Perhaps you are tempted to skip this chapter. I know I was. Aging happens to other people, not to us. Not yet, anyway. There will be plenty of time to think about it—later.

But better habits and better health care means that many of us will have a long second half of life. We may start out with energy and drive, but aging will slow us down. It's better than the alternative! So how can we plan for it?

When I interviewed these nine women, they ranged in age from seventy-two to eighty-two, so aging was a top-of-mind issue.

THE QUESTION

What have you learned, from your own experience and that of your friends, about the best frame of mind for facing aging and health declines?

Jane

Now, at the age of eighty, I am entering a time that I have likened to adolescence in a way because physical characteristics are changing. It's little things like not being able to turn pages of a book the way

I want to. Grasping things causes me sudden pain. But there's also this realization that I've entered elderdom. I cannot bring up words or names as quickly as I would like. Remembering things has been one of my prides. I can't count on doing that.

I'm also trying to make more of an effort to listen to my husband. There are things that we haven't talked about often, and we tend to have an attitude of "Don't worry about it, I'm okay." For example, "My leg may collapse when I get out of bed, but I'm okay, don't worry about it!" I'm trying to be a little more aware of how things are for him and also find ways to enter into conversation that isn't threatening. You would think that we would have worked that all out, but I find that it still needs work. It's a trick how to invite information without seeming to deliver a judgment.

This is a piece of wisdom I've learned: I am more aware of the need to be accepting of people whose ideas and reactions may be different than mine. I've found it helpful to wait and listen more during interactions with other people. I used to talk to my sister on the phone and do a crossword puzzle at the same time. Isn't that awful! Now I'm better at waiting and listening. It's part of the way I try to live with Richard, too.

I'm in a bit of self-denial. I am going to be facing tough times. There are changes that are happening in our life that I need to acknowledge—Richard's condition and my condition. Should I ask for a hip replacement or should I tough out this arthritic hip? Should I press Richard to get a hearing aid or should I just shout at him?

I feel very much my connection with the Holy and also the support and presence of people who walk that path with me. That is the way I look at our church congregation. I am in a support group there. I feel supported and sustained by my daughters and my sense of God's presence in life.

It's an interesting time of life. I'm aware of the past in an interesting way; sometimes it interferes and sometimes it is helpful.

But I'm also convinced that I need to spend more time on the present. I need to focus on what's happening now with the people around me—family, friends, and neighbors. That is one of my goals for my eighties: being more aware of the present. I try to be aware of my own body and my limitations, and of what's going on with Richard, the kids, and friends who are going through rough times, too.

Isabelle

The fear of old age is that someone will have to take care of you and you won't be able to do for yourself. How you get around that I don't know. You don't want to run out of money. You don't want to be dependent on anybody, but you fear you might be.

You just have to live from day to day and hope your body stays together. My friends and I have been talking a lot about what to do now. Do you move into a retirement home? You don't want to give up your lifestyle, and yet what happens when they take your car away and you can't drive? This has to be the most frightening time of life.

When I went to my college reunion, I listened to all these eighty-one-year-old women who still lived in their houses, and they were talking about dishes and furniture. One was even remodeling her house, and another was remodeling her kitchen. They weren't even thinking about moving. They were all in pretty good health, except for one, and she told us she was losing some of her memory. I thought that would be devastating. She was going to live with her daughter. I said, "How does that feel for you?" She said, "Well, I'll have my own room." She seemed to be okay with it. To me, it would just be awful.

All my friends are still driving on the freeway. One friend drove five hours in one day so she could be with us at the reunion. I don't like to get on freeways. I suppose part of it is because of the awful wreck my friend and I had with a logging truck. So far, that's the only limiting thing that I've found. But it's not limiting very much. I just take the back roads.

I keep saying, "When the time comes, I'll just put rocks in my pocket like Virginia Woolf and walk into the water." My friends say,

"Oh no. When you get there, you won't want to let go." That's probably true. I don't know how you face it.

Pamela

The loss of some things in life is really hard. When I was sixty-five, I thought aging would be a piece of cake. But actually living through diminished abilities is not that much fun. It shows up as physical problems, and everybody has their own. Mine happens to be arthritis. I talk to myself and say, *Buck up! It could be worse.* But it still hurts.

Also, my memory is going away. I've never had a real good memory, so I had to start making notes and writing things down to help me keep track of things. But that's getting to be more of a challenge.

Eating! I could eat anything, but now there are certain things that bother my stomach. I'm eliminating foods to see what it is. That's pretty big. I'm figuring it out.

One of the helpful things was watching my husband's mother grow older and change; she died at ninety-seven. Then watching my mother. She was a strong-willed woman, and in some ways she aged pretty well. In other ways, she did not face it. She said, "I will *not* move out of this house." I found out a little bit later that she didn't want to move because she didn't think she'd live very long! She was ninety before she moved. Like my mother-in-law, she also died at ninety-seven.

My sister and I wanted her to see alternative places to live. She'd say, "Oh, that's so lovely! Oh, that would be nice! I'm not going there." We planted the seed, but she refused to move until she was ready to acknowledge that she needed to move. She sat us both down and told us, "I think it's time. This house is getting too big." Well, we knew that fifteen years earlier. I'll tell you, you've never seen two sisters move so fast!

Here's what I learned from that: Don't wait till you're ninety. You've got to do things before the crisis happens. There can be a crisis at *any* time. My husband and I have been together on this, thank goodness. We're planning for our next stage of life. That doesn't mean it's easy. We made the decision to put our name on the waiting list for a retirement community. We've applied, and we've been accepted, provided we sell our house for enough.

One thing I really loved about my mother is that she had her will and all that stuff taken care of. She and Dad purchased cemetery plots in their younger years. Dad died suddenly at forty-seven, so they used the plot earlier than planned. To have that all taken care of was great. All we had to do was call the funeral home, and they came and got her. It was all paid for. So she was a good role model in that way. That's what we've been trying to do, make sure that all of our business is taken care of.

Being in denial is such a comfy place. But the ramification of being in denial can be hard. Our aunt, who is ninety-one now, said, "I will not move out of this apartment." Well, last summer she had an accident in a parking lot. Fortunately, she didn't run over anybody, but she wrecked her car. Then her life was in crisis. She hadn't even *thought* what she'd do if she didn't drive. She was ninety-one! And she had glaucoma! That accident really upset her, and pretty soon she was having trouble breathing, so they sent her to the hospital. Her daughter came here from Colorado and moved her to a new place. This independent woman who had said, "I won't do it any other way than my way!" had no choice. That's the ramification of being in denial.

Katherine

I feel receptive. Seriously. Grateful and receptive. You've got to be receptive because you don't know what will be around the corner. Gratitude helps a lot.

I have a friend who told me about a woman she knew who was very active. This woman lived across the street from a lake. When she started to fail, as an older woman, she would get out there and totter around. She got so she could just go a little ways before she had to come back and go home. Finally, she got so she could only sit in front of the window and look at the lake. She would still say, "Look at that bird over there." She seemed to be grateful for whatever was there in front of her that she could enjoy. I think that's what it takes. God knows if I have it.

Nobody gets out of here alive, so sooner or later each of us is going to keel over or we're going to have "the diagnosis." We don't get to choose either what diagnosis we'll have or when.

Another good friend is a retired Episcopal priest. He has spent a lot of time thinking about the period after active retirement and before death. He says there are certain questions you have to answer in those years: "Does my life have meaning?" and "What's the source of my hope?" What he's talking about would be good answers to your questions. My own response is receptivity and gratitude.

Susan

You need to realize that you are not going to get out of here alive, and you had better start planning. For example, we bought long-term health-care insurance before we were fifty-five. It was cheaper at that point. It's not going to pay us a whole lot, but it will help a little bit.

We started looking at retirement communities in the latter part of our fifties and early sixties. We wanted to have some choice and some idea of what we were going to be doing. We were on the waiting lists of three retirement places. We moved into one earlier this year.

I guess it's about being pragmatic. We always try to be very realistic about looking at what we have to do, what resources we have, what we can do, and what we can't do. We have never had what I would call a lavish life. We've never had a bunch of toys. We pay our credit cards off each month. We want to be solvent. We got our kids through college with no debt; that, we felt, was very important.

Part of living is realizing that you age daily. You've got to take the long view and say, "Are we both going to be here forever? Probably not. How can we make it easier for whoever is left?" It's all very well to say, "We're going to live forever" or "We're both going to die at the same time tomorrow." But that's probably not going to happen.

I'm sure we will miss a bunch of stuff as we go along. We can't anticipate everything; we can't meet all the eventualities before they happen. But you try to see what you can do. You have to realize that you can't predict what's going to happen, so you just have to prepare the best you can for what the future holds.

Eva

I think it helps to face aging with a sense of humor. It helps if we do our best to live healthfully, make the most of the time given, don't fear death, and don't go to extreme measures to prolong life, especially if its quality is seriously diminished.

Joy

So here I sit now, nearly eighty, alone, and deciding by myself what I'm going to do next. Do I have a road map? No. My choice is either to stay where I am now, living independently in a condo overlooking a quiet bay, or do something else. The question is what?

What will I do if/when I have a serious health issue that requires live-in help, which is extremely expensive? You're safe if you're in a retirement home and signed up for ongoing care before you get really sick or disabled. Most of us will have to face that issue; that's just reality! That's the big problem that people my age are trying to decide. The safe thing to do is to move into a retirement community early on. It's a unique and difficult question of how to plan your coming declining years.

I think I have learned from some experience to face aging and health declines. Right now, the declines are relatively minor and normal—failing eyesight, diminished hearing, and arthritis. I do not know how gracefully I'm doing it. What I do know is that there is no alternative to declining health and strength. Sure, you recognize that, and then embark on a career of going to a lot of doctors in an attempt to stay healthy. You get your exercise, your sleep, your pills. Unrealistically perhaps, we expect to conclude a wonderful life with growing "wonderfully old."

So at the moment, here's my decision: I will select a place to move—hopefully before I become frail so that my children will be spared the problems of "managing Mother's situation." When the time comes for me to go into a senior living residence, I'm going to treat it as if I am going to college. Remember, back when you were eighteen, you looked at college as a period of years of community living, fun, and education. You looked forward to all kinds of educational and social experiences, right? I'm going to look at the next stage as the University for New Life. Who knows what I will learn and discover there in my eighties and nineties? Whatever happens, here I come.

Ruth

I feel very positive about aging. That may change, but I find it to be a wonderful time of life. Part of that, I can say, is because my health at this point is good. That seems to be, I think, a large part about how you feel about aging. I've had scares, but that just makes you feel luckier and more grateful to God to be here.

I love this time of life because I think it's a very freeing time. We can be more who we are than we have been. I did turn eighty this year—which everyone at the church knows because Paul announced it! There's a sense for me—and probably anyone else at this age—that we need to do some of the things that we have wanted to do. I've always wanted to go back to New England to see some of the friends my first husband and I made at Yale whom I've not seen in all these years, and to see New England in the fall again. At first I thought, *Oh we can't do that now.* But I broached it to Paul, and we're on our way.

Also, I've joined a new writing group. We call ourselves Women of a Certain Age. There are six of us, all younger than I am, all published, accomplished poets. We encourage and affirm each other. I'm writing and doing a lot of revision, too, which is pleasing to me because I'm confident enough now to know that I want to change a poem. Even though I love the poem, I can see ways to make it better.

I'm convinced that living a long life enhances and enriches us.

MY TAKEAWAYS

Denial. Acceptance. Fear. Gratitude. Hard choices. Practical tips. Pain. Receptivity. Diminished abilities. A freeing time of life. A chance to do things you always wanted to do.

What more can I say? We all have our own attitudes and learnings.

I'll end with Ruth's words:

"As long as I'm feeling good and as long as my mind is working, I think this age is good, very good. To be alive; it's sheer luck."

Chapter 16

Moving on from Loss

THE LONGER WE live, the more loss we have to cope with. Some of us are lucky enough to get through childhood without losing any friends, parents, or siblings—and without the grief of a divorce in the family. But even children and young people have losses. Friends move away. The family relocates and leaves behind a beloved house. Flood or fire damages or destroys our treasured stuff. Accidents happen. Illness strikes out of the blue. As adults, many of us have to learn what it is to lose a job, our savings, or our dreams.

I've heard it said that everyone copes with loss differently, and there is no right way or wrong way to grieve. But I've also seen people who cannot seem to get over their losses. After a period of grieving, it seems sensible to find a new direction or meaning or purpose in life, to keep moving forward. Yet some people cannot seem to find any direction or meaning, and they seem stuck in misery and self-pity.

What's the key? What is it that helps some people to move on?

THE QUESTION

How were you able to move on after a deep loss in your life? What have you learned about ways to cope with personal loss?

Susan

In your forties and fifties, you begin to see more of the sadness or tragedies in life. At that point some of your friends are getting divorced, and some of them have kids who are in real trouble. Some of them, or their husbands, have lost a job, or their savings are used up, or they don't have anything to look forward to in their retirement years. If you have not been able to put anything into your retirement by the time you're forty or fifty, you jolly well better start.

All of those things start to be real in your forties and fifties. They become even more real in your sixties, because in those years people that you loved and cared for—like your parents, aunts, and uncles—are dying. You are beginning to face death and severe illness and loss of all kinds of things. You have to learn how to deal with those losses and how to climb out of the hole that you find yourself in during those times.

Both my husband and I are pragmatists, and that helps. We don't always succeed. But when something's going to happen or we're going to make a decision, we try to look at all the options. We try to look at the very worst outcome that could possibly happen with that particular thing. Then we work backward. To us, it's easier if we spread all the options out and look at them as clearly as we can. If it is a financial situation, go to somebody who has some financial expertise to explain the options. If it's a physical thing, do the same with a physician. If it's a family thing, then try to lay out all the options that you have before you. You have to try very hard to get your ducks in a row.

One friend's husband died about three months ago, and he had put together a notebook of all the things she had to do if he died. That has been terribly helpful to her. She didn't have to bumble through but could think clearly, step by step, *These are the things I have to do.*

It's the old Boy Scout motto, "Be prepared."

Ruth

When Tom and I divorced, in a very generous gesture, he deeded our old house to me. My daughter, Sara, and I were able to stay there until I retired, but maintenance of it had to be minimal. We lived through flooding, damaging windstorms, even pestilence in the form of hordes of carpenter ants that ate away several walls and our entire downstairs bathroom. I am aware that it was a lot for my young daughter to handle, but thanks to friends and neighbors and our own hard work, we made it through. And we even found a way to have those walls rebuilt!

One very helpful thing—this is true of all of my children, and a lot of it is from their dad—is a sense of humor, oftentimes black humor. I am thankful for that. We did a lot of laughing through our hard times, too—crying and laughing. What it did to this little girl, how it changed and molded her, I can only guess. Sara was definitely way wise before her time and terribly sensitive to everything that happened. That she is the deeply caring, happy-spirited person that she is today is a tribute to her—and to God's faithfulness.

Katherine

It helps me if I can acknowledge my loss, and not all losses can be acknowledged. I just had a very dear friend move out of town; she's my golfing buddy and a writing buddy. We've had a lot of time to talk. We'd look each other in the eye and say, "This is hard. I can hardly stand it that you're not going to be available the way that we're used to." Just acknowledging how hard it will be is going to help, I think.

I've made a point of acknowledging the loss of my marriage and having some conversations with Ben where both of us were able to say we miss each other. I think we will love each other for the whole rest of our lives. We've been able to acknowledge it without going over the top and thinking we've made a terrible mistake. It would be awful if we got back to together again; I can't imagine.

Still, there are kinds of losses—the loss of a baby, the loss of a parent—where you just put one foot in front of the other and plod through the period that it takes to get used to it. Of course, it doesn't hurt that you can always look around and see people with unimaginably worse losses than anything that you've experienced. Not to be Pollyannaish about it, but there is that.

Loss is a natural part of life. If you live long enough you are going to experience loss. You don't get out without it.

My mother had a dear friend, whom I always knew as Aunt Grace. Her daughter Sally was found dead next to her car one day. Nobody knew whether she was in an accident or whether she overdosed on some stuff she was taking and just fell out of her car in a stupor and died. Aunt Grace was never the same again. Her timeframe was always "before Sally…" and "after Sally . . ." I knew that the ". . ." stood for "died."

I've been so blessed. I've taken advantage of opportunities to learn, like the "Sophia" work that I did, a workshop about "the five seasons." There are always new beginnings, the flowering, as in spring. Some aspect of life comes to fruition, and you harvest in late summer. Then you go into fall, which is all about loss, and then winter, where you think nothing is going to happen. And while it looks like nothing is going on in the garden, the bulbs you've cut back are under there, ready to pop out in the spring. We like spring, and we like late summer, the harvest. Then we want to jump right over to spring, again, skipping winter.

If you're stuck in any season of life, you go back to the season before. You ask yourself, *Did I really do the work here?* For instance, letting go is a natural part of autumn. Sometimes you can't let go because you haven't really acknowledged the harvest.

When Ben and I were going through our divorce, we met with our counselor. We asked each other for forgiveness, and then we asked for the gifts. That was her design. She said, "If you don't do a decent job of acknowledging the fruits of the harvest of this marriage, you two will never be able to let go and move on. It's not going to save you from the grief. But if you don't do that and you divorce, you might never be able to get out of the downward spiral."

The work of fall, the grieving part, is cleaning out and pruning for the sake of life.

For example, my friend Millie's husband died a couple of years ago, and she just announced to her kids that she's selling the house and moving to a townhouse. One of her kids said, "Oh, good! That's great for you." The other said, "But that's our home." Millie told her kids, "Yes, that's our home, but I feel burdened by it. I feel burdened by the size of it. I feel burdened by the expense of it. I feel burdened by all the stuff. I want to move forward, lighter in my life. I had happy memories in that house, but we will create happy memories in the place that I'm moving to." These kids are grown boys, married.

I admire that ability of hers, to see a different vision and to shed the stuff that's weighing her down. I think that's marvelous wisdom, and it's not mine.

Anna

I didn't learn to grieve when I was a child. Mother didn't know how to do that. When we moved again and again, there was no goodbye to where we were before we left. It was a positive thing, in that she said there was always something good that we were going to get to do next. "Won't this be fun?" she'd say. But we ignored letting go.

Part of my therapy was grieving all the losses I experienced, the abuse, the moving, and the parenting that was not as there as it could've been. I had to learn about grief.

Then through education, conferences, and classes, I became a grief counselor. I've led classes for certified nurse's aides, hospital and convalescence aides, and others, teaching about grief and loss. I had the privilege of leading grief support groups and working closely with individual people. At the hospital, I started a bereavement program.

I teach that it is the norm to grieve, that it is healthy and very important to acknowledge when we've experienced loss and pay attention to it—not shove it down or ignore it. It's important to do it in a way that works best for us. There is no right way or wrong way.

I have a lot I can say about grief and loss. I didn't know how to do it; I do now. I'm very grateful for that learning, probably more than any other learning because aging is about loss, number one. We're going to have to move and leave our big house one of these days. My husband is aging, rapidly. Saying goodbye to our parents was difficult. A dear friend of fifty years just moved to Southern California to be closer to her daughter. Loss is half of life, and if we don't deal with it, the other half isn't any good. If we know how to grieve, we gain. Grief attended to brings wisdom.

Grief shoved under the carpet is going to come out some way or another, perhaps someday in a health issue. As a chaplain, I noticed that at least half the patients had another issue, besides their medical problem, that was bigger for them. They'd say something like, "But what's really bothering me is . . ." And it would be something major, such as "I had to move from my house of thirty years because my husband died," "I'm still having Vietnam flashbacks," or "My middle son won't have anything to do with me." It comes out as a physical ailment. Grief does not go away. And everyone's body reflects grief in a unique way.

Even worse is overarching grief—a whole bunch of grief at one time, like when your family dies in a fire and you're the sole survivor. Wow. I think it would be amazing for someone not to get ill after experiencing something that traumatic. How can one manage that kind of a huge loss? People do have to go through traumas like that, and I'm amazed by the people who are able to do it. But generally they don't do it without, at the very least, getting a bad cold. More often something worse, such as cancer, heart disease, stomach problems, psychological problems, or relational problems.

I have seen some people who just never get over their grief. These are usually people who don't try. They remain stuck in their memories, thinking, *I don't want to let go.* Most people find a way, at least moderately, to move on—some with great difficulty, others with some ease. You don't ever know for sure who's going to do it or how because everybody's different. You don't know what their learning is already. If they've never learned to grieve before, it's a whole new deal. Sometimes old grief will come up and fill their plate to overflowing, along with the new one. It can be challenging, even overwhelming.

Grief counseling is a really important thing to have available to people.

MY TAKEAWAYS

Not long after I recorded the above insights, my mother died at the age of ninety-two. She lived a good, long life and did not suffer long. Still, her passing left a hole in my heart. It helped me to review some of the wisdom I heard from these women I admire:

+ "Loss is half of life, and if we don't deal with it, the other half isn't any good."

+ "It is very important to acknowledge when we've experienced loss and pay attention to it—not shove it down or ignore it."

+ Grief unattended to can bring on physical illness. Grief attended to brings wisdom.

+ Sometimes you have to let go of all your stuff.

+ "Grieving is a season of life, like fall. The work of fall is cleaning out and pruning for the sake of life. Spring will come again, and you need to be ready to welcome it."

Chapter 17

Preventing Regrets

WOULDN'T IT BE great if you could sit down now with your future self and ask, "What are your greatest regrets?" What if you could prevent those regrets by making a decision and acting now?

Hindsight is always 20/20, and none of these women has the same life you do. But for me, it's eye-opening to hear what they have to say about regrets.

This may be the best way to get advice from an older person: find out what she regrets and how she might have done things differently. After that, though, it's up to you.

THE QUESTION

What do you wish you had done differently, particularly in your forties and fifties? What regrets do you have?

Pamela

I do have regrets. But I hope that I've limited them because I try to do things to ensure I won't have too many.

For instance, my mother and I never had a very good relationship. At one point in my life, I just said, "I'm going to have to bite the bullet and see her, because I don't want to regret when she's gone." I'd leave her house crying because she would say hurtful things to me. But I had the tenacity to go back. And every time I started over, I didn't labor over what the last issue was. I let it be. I actually turned that relationship around. She finally learned to like me.

I do regret one thing. I had expectations for the kids. When they didn't behave or wouldn't do things like I thought they should, I would get mad at them. But in the end, we had our talk and our hugs; then we'd start over. I wish I had been able to do that differently.

I can say now to families, when their kids are four or five years old, "You know, they're not very old. They are still learning. It's their job to do that, and your job to guide them." But I didn't quite get that when my kids were little.

Jane

If I were doing it differently, I would have made more of an effort to see my parents. I think I missed a bit in that. Now, as I get older, that time spent with my brothers and sisters seems more precious. Certainly, I would encourage people: don't let time with your family go.

On the other hand, I didn't always love being with my family of origin because of conflicts that were going on—sometimes between my parents and sometimes between my siblings and them. There were times when I felt, *Oh, I can't take on that burden of listening to my mother go through this again!* and *Can I really take a week of my sister-in-law?* So you see, when I think, *I wish I had spent more time with family*—there were reasons I didn't. I think most people have these. I probably missed some good things by not making the effort to go there.

My sister lived in California, and she used to go back to our hometown in Minnesota and camp there for weeks and weeks in the summer. I never did that. She had a stronger attachment there. It's interesting to me now to talk with my sister. We spend more time now than we ever did talking about the past and the present.

A lot of my time living here, thousands of miles from where I grew up, has been feeling free of family. I can appreciate my family now, but they could be difficult. I don't think they're any different than most families. Well, some families have probably done it with more grace.

Eva

I regret that my marriage ended. I wish that I had understood my husband better. I would love to have been happily married to him forever. But the way things were, that couldn't be. And good things have come about since, so I have much to be thankful for.

Susan

Every once in a while I'll say I wish I hadn't done so-and-so. Then I think, *I can't change that now. It's really dumb to beat myself up for it.* We all do stuff that we wish we hadn't. I can think of several things that I've done that I wish I hadn't. But then I think of King David and the way God dealt with him. Even though David was great, he really did some bad things. Yet he was sorry for what he did, and God used him anyway.

We have to remember that. God loves us regardless. It's for us to forgive ourselves to some degree for the stupid things we do. God forgives us, but we have to forgive ourselves and not spend the rest of our life wishing we hadn't done it.

Isabelle

Looking back, I wish I had more training in acting. I didn't think about it at the time. I wish I had done that in college or afterwards, but I didn't.

I had fun in high school and college. I loved both of them. But I wasn't really a student; I was having fun. I wish I had been more of a student. Now I read a lot of things, and I ask people if they've heard of the author. I'm finally starting to catch up, reading wonderful authors I never read before, such as Iris Murdoch and A. S. Byatt.

Also, I always wanted to go to Paris. My mother was born there. Sam and I were going to do that and then he got sick. I regretted that for a long time. But then, after Sam died, my daughter Annie and I finally went. We even saw Monet's garden. It was wonderful.

Joy

A pastor friend told me that when he visits someone who is dying, he often asks if they have regrets and what regrets they have. His goal is to help the dying person, and he hears all kinds of answers. He told me that my husband was one of the very few people who answered, "No, I have no regrets." Jeff went on to describe to the pastor—and this was absolutely tear-jerking for me—how blessed he was in life, career, and family, that he had absolutely no regrets.

My forties and fifties were a time when I finished with my job as a mother, and I essentially had completed a lot of the community things I did because they were related to the kids. Thereafter I focused on a totally different thing: going to seminary and researching creativity and women. I got into the whole issue of women's rights, which has enriched me so much. Actually, I have no regrets from my forties and fifties because I chose this time to move on.

Perhaps if I do have one regret, it is that I went along with the cultural norm of my time, and did not push outside of those societal boundaries of the 1950s. I acted within expectations of girls and women for my time. To have done otherwise would probably not have been authentic for me, given my upbringing. I also went to a traditional, small, church-related college, and I felt loved and appreciated there, but I also began to feel the limited opportunity that was expected of girls after graduation.

Why did I not rebel? Well, I was pretty happy with what I was doing, and I was in love with a wonderful man, and we were getting married. It was true there was no funding for me to go to grad school at that time, anyway. Then the kids came, and with that lots of challenge, change, and learning, all of which made me happy.

Nowadays, I do admire those who moved out of the norm, in spite of the barriers for women. But truly I feel no sour grapes. So I guess I really have no serious regrets. Those were just "my times." I did my best, and I have had a really good life.

Katherine

I don't know if this is a regret. If regret is "I didn't do this and I wish I had," I'd say figure out whatever it takes to listen to yourself. For me, that came about through writing or being by myself. If I have a question on my mind and I sit down with a journal and start writing, I write myself to the answer. Then once you've got it, honor it.

I now realize there were several different places in my life where at some level I knew I should "leave this job" or that "Being with this woman feels like home." Yet it took me so long to get my head and my gut together that I wasted a lot of time. There were always other things that distracted me.

I would say, "Listen to yourself." If you don't start doing it when you're in your forties and fifties, when will you? I mean you might start when you're in your sixties or seventies, and that would be better than never having done it at all. But for the sake of honesty and the fullness of your life, get to it as soon as you can. And then don't be afraid. Nobody is perfect, and there isn't any one law about how we're supposed to live our lives.

If you have a little thing in your gut that's giving you a message—do whatever it takes to listen to it fully. Test it inside yourself. This is a very introverted process I'm talking about. An extrovert would need to get a group together and say, "This is what I'm thinking about. What do you think? Give me your ideas. Help me test this." But whatever it would take, if you get a glimmering and think this is true for you, do what you can to test it out. And if it really is true for you—act on it.

Marie brought a quote from Thoreau to that first workshop where I met her. It's in her room even now. It says, "If I'm not I, who am I to be?"

MY TAKEAWAYS

If you're in your forties or fifties, what can you do to avoid regrets?

These women offered many suggestions: Try to understand your husband and children better. Keep in touch with your parents and your siblings, even if they drive you crazy. Get more training in something you love. Take that special trip, if you can. Try something new and different.

And most importantly—find a way to listen to yourself and then honor what you hear. Don't put it off, waste time, or get distracted. Get to it as soon as you can. Make this a priority. If you're not living a life that fulfills you and satisfies you, figure out why. And then change things—before it's too late.

Chapter 18

Evolving Faith

I WASN'T SURE WHETHER or not to include a question about faith. These days it's politically incorrect to talk about religion. Christianity has gotten a bad name from a few outspoken, narrow-minded people who use it as a lash to whip the marginalized—surely not the intention of its founder. And many people who kept the faith for years have found themselves harmed or appalled by the policies of their own churches. But from my perspective, inside a welcoming, open-minded church, I can see a different sort of Christianity, the kind that doesn't make headlines—the kind that makes people examine their lives and their values and try to act accordingly.

Although I was raised in the church—Presbyterian as it happens—I stopped attending at the age of fifteen and was "unchurched" for twenty years. At college, I picked up the message that smart people didn't believe in all that religious stuff. Science couldn't prove it. Anthropologists claimed that humans made it all up to explain the unknown. I bought into these ideas. I went gallivanting around the world, certain that the church was irrelevant.

When I moved back to the States, with a husband and baby, I found and joined a neighborhood church, mainly for community. Far away from my extended family, I wanted my child to grow up amid a supportive group of "grandmas" and "cousins" and learn about her heritage from my side of the family. At first, I had no faith at all. Then I started listening and learning. I went to classes and helped invite speakers. I read books. As it happened, I had stumbled upon a particularly broad-minded, progressive congregation.

I discovered that the church—at least some parts of it—was changing. In almost every denomination, long-held assumptions were being examined. Women were stepping up to take leadership roles. Doubts were welcomed and discussed openly. That old exclusive attitude— "This is the only path to salvation and nobody else is getting into heaven"—was evolving into a search for transformation to a better way of living, as individuals and with each other. At my church, we invited speakers of other faiths to explain their beliefs and traditions to us, especially after 9/11. I began to feel more and more comfortable in this church. As I looked around, I recognized growing wisdom in many of the members, men and women, young and, especially, old.

The nine women quoted in this book were people I met through my church. Most of them—though not all!—answered these tough questions from a central core of faith. Whether or not they can explain it—and most of them can—this faith gives them strength, solace, and perspective. Although some readers may find this aspect of their advice irrelevant, I decided not to censor their responses.

Most of these women admit that their faith has changed over the years. As children, they accepted what they were taught in Sunday school. Their churches offered firm answers, not thoughtful choices. The only choice was "Take it or leave it." But as they grew, read, and experienced life, their faith deepened and transformed into something new. Committed to lifelong learning, they delved into new interpretations of the gospel. They began to understand things in new ways.

In the 1960s, when their church started accepting women in positions of responsibility, these women were the right age to take on these roles, so they became pioneers. In the Presbyterian Church, as in other mainline denominations, those in this generation were among the first women in their churches to accept the roles of elder (on the church's governing board, also known as session) and deacon (a position in charge of reaching out and caring for other members). Then the regional association of churches (the presbytery) and the national church also called on them, asking them to speak up and serve on committees. As the church evolved, they were in the forefront. So for many, the church was the safe venue where they unfolded their wings. Or not so safe.

Because I was outside the church for so long, my path was very different from theirs. I was curious to know how their faith had changed during their many decades of membership—and how it affected their answers to my questions.

THE QUESTION

How has faith informed or guided important moments and decisions? How has your faith changed over the years?

Pamela

That's a tough question. My parents took me to Sunday school and church from an early age, so I always had that church background. When I went to college, I stayed connected to the church and went to youth group. Then when I met my future husband, he was a church man. So all my life I have gone to church. I just believe. It's who I am.

I don't know how that religious thing melds together with my decisions, because it's all part of me. I don't know whether we took in foster children because of our religion, or if we would have done it anyway because we cared for kids. It's just such an integrated thing for me that I can't tell where the religion lets off and life begins.

Church gives me comfort; I just love to be in church. I miss it a lot when we don't go, which isn't very often; mostly when we're out of town. What matters most is the people there, who are so nurturing and wonderful, so accepting and caring. We started going to this church when we moved here, when I was twenty-two. So the old-timers today are people who were all young together. We all grew together.

The church has been instrumental in helping me grow in other ways too, through responsibilities and committee work, and I've found it to be a place where women are appreciated.

I definitely believe in God, and I go to that belief when I'm depressed—reading meditations or praying. I've gotten to the point where I know God can't solve everybody's problems. He's given us free will, so there aren't a lot of answers. But that, too, is helpful—to know that each one of us has our own journey, and we're all in a different place.

Eva

My faith continues to change and grow.

When I was a young child during World War II, my father served in the Canadian army overseas for more than four years. My brother, my mother, her mother, and I lived a very quiet life in a little house just around the corner from an Anglican church. Church was where the excitement was. Sunday school, intriguing Bible stories, crafts, friends, picnics, music, parties, visits from Santa, grainy black-and-white movie cartoons, church services with robust and beautiful organ music, a magnificent white-robed choir who looked and sounded to me like angels. I loved it all. I loved Sundays because that was the day when "I get to go to church!"

Later in life, there came a time when I felt, "I should go to church," and for a while, "I don't think I need church." When we had our children, I wanted them to experience church, enjoy Sunday school and the friendship of kids their own age getting together and gaining a sense of God and faith in their lives. We visited a few churches, but we didn't feel that we "belonged" in them—until a friend directed us to the church to which I still belong. Now, once again I'm delighted whenever "I get to go to church!"

Today, my understanding of God is much different from that which I held as a child. I believe in a personal God—not in God who is a person, but God who is personal to me. I believe that here on earth, God is Spirit. I expect that that Spirit is at work in ways that may be different in each of us. That Spirit loves and nourishes each of us in such a way that we may best "live and move and have our being," as the Bible says. Just how that works is a mystery to me.

My relationship to Jesus is changing too. These days I take Jesus as my brother—not so much as my personal Lord and Savior. When Jesus asks us to pray "Our Father," that, to me, means that he sees us as siblings. And scripture informs that we are "heirs together with Christ," hence, we're family. Also, artist Dudley Carter introduced me to the branch of Christianity he followed, the Christadelphians, who describe themselves as brothers and sisters in Christ. Learning about them got me thinking about our kinship with Jesus and with each other. I don't believe that this idea of Jesus as our brother is irreverent or sacrilegious. It's not diminishing Christ in my mind and in my heart to consider him that way. It helps me a lot.

Christian Scientist friends have told me that they understand the Christ to be, not the personality of Jesus of Nazareth, but the eternal might of Godliness that was behind his ministry. I like that. It makes me think that if I can't see Christ in, for example, my loving, devout Muslim friends—Jihad and Farida—I'll never recognize him.

Anna

I learned my faith from my mother. Most children emulate parents or family faith to start with. In her church, which was High Episcopal, what I learned was "God is distant, and if you're a good girl, everything will be fine." You say "thank you" when things go well. And you belong in church every Sunday and sing in the choir. Singing was a joy for her as she grew up with her dad, and I loved it, too. She taught me to be involved in the church but did not teach a deep understanding of the why of it.

After college, there was a period of time when I, like many young people, drifted away from the church. My husband was very uncomfortable in the Episcopal Church because it was too Roman. He'd grown up Methodist, so we attended Presbyterian or Methodist or whatever was handy. Then I was busy having babies, five in a row, so Sunday became just another busy day. At some point, I remember promising God I would get us to church at least once a month if...I forget what the "if" was. I think it was if my husband got a new job. I kept to that commitment, though it wasn't hard because I was comfortable being in church.

When we moved to this area in 1960 again, my life was just busyness; I couldn't keep up. Finally when the kids were big enough, I went to church pretty regularly. At that church, when I would go to worship, I had the sense of being able to climb up on a fence and look over the top. I could see what was really good on the other side. Then when I went home, I had to climb back down again. I was catching a glimpse of something that I hadn't seen before.

Then we moved to a nearby town and joined a different church. That pastor led us through some excellent Bible studies, so I actually got acquainted with the Bible. He taught about justice too, which I had never considered as being part of the gospel. It was from there that I began to feel the call to ministry.

My relationship with God is an underpinning of who I am and all that I am. It's just a basic assumption that God is with me all the time, and that I can turn to God. God understands grief and loss. God understands joy, and God is with me.

However, I have to say I'm pretty marginally Christian anymore about who Jesus is, what "the Christ" means, and how literal all of the scripture is. To me, Christianity is about love. The central message is about how God loves us. I have always believed that from the inside out. I've never questioned that.

My faith has changed big time. I now believe that God isn't a superior being monitoring our behaviors; faith is about relationship and who I am. As I became more certain about my own worth, I could relate to God in a new way. That is a key for all people in a relationship with God: how they perceive themselves and the authority figures in their lives.

For many women, it is impossible to think of God as male because men have been the source of abuse, neglect, or abandonment. When I was counseling, if I saw that was the case, I urged a woman to find a new word for God.

Once I was working with a patient who was deeply disturbed. I had had a long phone conversation with this individual, late at night. After it ended, I had to let go and lie down and go to sleep. I sat up again, worried deeply about this person because I didn't know what he was going to do to himself. Suddenly, I had this image of a woman, there, available, waiting for me. She wanted me to come and put that person in her arms. She told me she was Gramma-God. She was strong, wise, in charge, and understanding. She said, "This is my problem, not yours. I'll take care of this person; you don't have to. You go back to sleep now." So now, when things are really tough, that image is an easy place for me to go. It was a very solid, powerful experience that I had, because afterward I relaxed and went to sleep.

I'm very adamant about inclusive language. I don't like referring to God as "he" or "him." I don't even like to say, "Lord." I substitute the word "God" a good deal of the time, in songs and everything else. That word, "Lord," wrecks the sense of relationship. I can't believe it's an up-down relationship. It's not a ruler-ruled relationship.

To me, Gramma-God offers strength and wisdom and the capacity to handle whatever difficulties arise—in a way that is absolutely secure. It was an amazing experience. It was a gift and a treasure.

Isabelle

I've had a strange experience with faith. My mother was Catholic, but she didn't raise us as Catholics because some priest came around and told her my father wasn't truly married to her because he wasn't a Catholic. That was the end of that.

Instead, she sent us to the Christian Science Church with a friend of hers. As the years went on, I kept up with it; even in high school I would go to different events. My parents weren't religious whatsoever. I'd get up on Sunday and go to church; nobody else would.

Then I met Sam at college. He was a Methodist, and he was very active in his church. He went to all the youth groups and even went back East to a youth conference. So I started going to church with him. But I wasn't baptized until after I was married.

When we were in San Francisco, we went to a very active social-justice church. I was baptized in that church. Sam was in the army; he and I led Sunday school classes. I did it because it was part of his life. But I always had trouble understanding the doctrine of the church, including the virgin birth, even the resurrection.

Every time we moved, we went to different churches. We were Lutherans for a while, Methodists, and then Presbyterians. For me, it was an instant community. I think it was for him, too, because he also had all kinds of doubts. We started going to this church in 1963 when we first moved to this area. Our neighbors took us. Sam became very active; he was the clerk of session and he managed the finances. I taught Sunday school, but I didn't like it very much. I did what I thought I was supposed to do.

And the faith—oh, I wish I knew, but I just don't know about that. I'm learning a lot, especially from people who seem to have a lot of faith. I want to know how I get that. I'm still trying to figure that part out. I don't even know about dying; I don't know if anything happens to you. Some people get so rabid about that sort of thing. How can everything be about getting to heaven when everything can be so wonderful here?

I'm too much of a questioner to have faith. I guess I don't.

Susan

My faith has broadened incredibly. It has grown and deepened and widened.

I was the most narrow-minded person. In those days, I didn't understand what I believe now: that when Jesus said, "Other sheep I have that are not of this fold," he meant it. He came for all of us; he didn't come just for the Presbyterians or for the Christians.

He tried to show us a way that all of us could live a better life. His sacrifice on the cross was not to save our sins, it was because he was showing us a way that the authorities of that time found dangerous. He was crucified because he was a rebel. He was threatening the establishment, and that establishment was very exclusive, not inclusive.

From my point of view, that's what it's all about. I was just sick when I read in the paper about the Sikh massacre in Wisconsin. Nobody can tell me it wasn't a hate crime.

I don't pray as much as I think I should, but I pray in very quick snatches during the day. Something will come to my mind and I'll just send off what we used to call a "bullet prayer."

Hopefully, I will continue to grow. That's what I'm trying very hard to do. That's why it's so important to me to think, read, learn, and be aware.

Katherine

I have always been interested in things relating to faith and religion. I like reading books that help explain things—books by Joan Chittister, Marcus Borg, and Bishop John Shelby Spong. I have always been fascinated by Barbara Brown Taylor and Karen Armstrong, who wrote about Islam and other religions. I've always been interested in the philosophy of life, in what's it all about.

Where I've come now is this: it's much more about God than about church. I have hung up my straps as a good church woman. I used to think that what the church thinks was what God thinks—until I got into conflict about that through my own life. I do think there is a place for the church, but the church is not God.

God can be found in the church, but God can also be found outside of the church, in many other places. The church can serve God, or the church can be a real huge institution for status quo or power domination. Living with someone who has been wounded by the Catholic Church the way Marie has, I don't think I'd ever be able to give my allegiance to the church and have it be a central place in my life the way it was for so long. Even a good church. I don't care to be on another committee. I just want to go to worship and be a ringer in the bell choir.

Sometimes when I go for a walk, when I think about how I can deal with a situation, I get an idea and I think it comes from God. I choose to say that. I think I'm in a pretty darn close partnership with God. I don't always hold up my end of it, but God is always there.

Joy

I was lucky to be raised by a Christian family, and I was happy to go to a Christian college and to be married to a wonderful Christian man. Jeff and I loved talking about the hard questions of faith. This was an area of our lives we enjoyed exploring together. Of course, I've had periods of doubt. Every thinking person has to question some of the things we have been taught. And there are numerous questions of religion that we should debate!

Early on in our church life, Jeff and I signed up to be leaders for our kids' youth group, and that required us to answer tough questions. It is not for the faint of heart! Then I did the master's program at San Francisco Theological Seminary, where I got to have meaningful discussions with professors and classmates. Becoming an elder and deacon also added to my spiritual renewal.

Now I do a number of things to keep my faith fresh and evolving. I go to church always, and I sing in the choir. This brings me great joy to be able to be a part of the worship. I also go to retreats regularly to keep my faith moving and growing. The church is the center of my life. And it works well even now that I am a single person. We are not forgotten. We are included and loved.

Ruth

Faith colors my life. It is endemic to my life. It has been a central part of my life from the time my mother taught me to sing "Blessed Assurance," when I was three or four. It's just there.

The worshipping community part of it is essential to me, the music, the prayers, the Word, the people. However, I'm not as interested in the institutional end of it—as they say, "Been there, done that."

When I have a decision to make, or when I'm going through a tough time, my prayer life expands. I am not terribly specific in my prayers. Author Anne Lamott says the most common prayers are "Help, help" and "Thanks, thanks." Certainly gratitude is the largest part of my praying—lots of "Thank you, thank you," with an occasional, fervent "Help!"

I didn't lose my faith during those difficult years. My faith is firmly planted. But it has definitely changed over the years. It has dramatically changed.

My parents were old-fashioned Methodists, what you would probably call fundamentalist. Their faith was more evangelical than mine, but they *are* the ones who set the bar for me, as far as growing up in God's hands. Though I could never buy some of the dogma, their living lessons of a loving God are still with me.

Being at Yale with Tom, my faith began to broaden. And being at my current church for more than fifty years, it has grown and expanded. Even in the last few years, I find that I'm looking at some really basic things differently.

To believe that other world religions have validity, that their followers are just as much on their path to God as we—that thought has been liberating for me. The heavy burden is gone. I wish I'd understood much sooner that God's love is truly universal and inescapable, *and* that judgment is God's alone.

Jane

My sense of the presence of God has definitely changed. Before, it was an academic knowledge; I used to ask questions like "What is the real historic meaning of this passage in scripture?" My questions have become "What does this say to me that might have spoken to people who wrote it and to people through the years who have read it? And what is the sustaining power behind that?" I'm still interested in the history of how the Bible was put together, and what those events would have looked like to our modern mentality. But now I have more of a sense of presence of God in scripture. I hesitate to use that language because it is so often misused or casually used. But I find I believe in that.

The church I grew up in is much different than the church I'm in now. I haven't always had an awareness of an immediacy of God in my life. What made that change was the realization that a personal relationship was available, if I accepted it. I now sense that more is being offered to me. It's there; it's for me. Faith is a relationship that I have, and it's a sustaining relationship.

When making decisions, or going through a tough time, I take it to prayer. It's more than just dumping it; I also think on it. I try not to put it out of mind. In the past, often I have been able to put aside concerns because I had something else to do, like run a meeting. Now, I'm trying to face up to what is really happening.

I try to find ways to talk about my concerns so that I'm getting some advice. If I do not shy away from interacting with the people involved—and this would be family—if I make a point of being more involved in their lives and their thoughts and do this in nonjudgmental, asking-for-help ways, I often find the answers are there and given by other family members. By nature I'm an introvert and not inclined to invite other people into my thoughts. But I find that when I do—this is one way prayer is answered. It comes through the people that we're trying to live with and love.

MY TAKEAWAYS

I was surprised to hear Isabelle say she doesn't have faith, after a lifetime of attending church. I was also surprised to hear Anna, who went to seminary and worked as a chaplain, say she is "pretty marginally Christian anymore about who Jesus is." For those who think all churchgoers walk in lockstep and are forced to believe exactly the same thing, this could serve as an eye-opener.

It was fascinating for me to hear how some of these women developed their own images of God and Jesus. The old guy with a white beard image is fading, as is the man on the cross with a halo. Eva admires Jesus as her big brother and feels compelled to declare this notion is "not irreverent or sacrilegious." Susan sees Jesus as a rebel who threatened the establishment. And Anna's image of Gramma-God is warm and comforting, nurturing and accepting in a way that Michelangelo's Sistine Chapel painting is not. To them, God is not distant and impersonal. Faith can be a sustaining relationship.

Prayer also takes on new meaning. When troubled, Katherine goes for long walks and when good ideas pop into her head, she thanks God. After all, neuroscience can't explain where good ideas come from. Jane finds her prayers answered when she opens herself up and invites her loved ones to give her advice.

Perhaps you will disagree with these notions or find them irrelevant. Perhaps you will catch a glimpse of something you had not seen before. Anyway, this is how these women see their own faith, and their insights and advice in other chapters rise from it.

Chapter 19

Making a Difference

"**Making a Difference**" is another rather grandiose chapter title; I hope you'll bear with me here. I wanted to ask about volunteer work, about giving back to the community. Increasingly, high schools are requiring students to perform a certain number of hours of volunteer work to qualify for graduation, and some corporations encourage their employees to teach skills in classrooms or mentor at-risk children. National television news shows highlight people who are "making a difference" by sending supplies to American troops or teaching music in the schools. Concern over the environment leads some to treat injured owls and release them back to the wild or donate to organizations conserving land for nature reserves.

When I hear this, I ask myself, *What more could I be doing to make a difference?* For a year or so, I tutored immigrants in basic English, because I know how hard it is to learn fluency in another language. I've taught writing and served on committees and tried to be there for friends in need. But I have this nagging sense that I should be doing more. Now that I'm in the second half of life, I feel I should be aiming higher—not just pursuing personal success but doing whatever small things I can to address some greater need, such as hunger or violence or poverty.

I want to do something to make the world a better place—to leave a legacy that's more than "She enjoyed life" or "She cared about the people she cared about." Yet what? The sages say all action begins with one person. In the second half of life, I have the time and resources to contribute to something larger than my personal well-being—something that could make my life more meaningful. What might that be?

Most of the women I interviewed have done a lot of volunteer work—far more than I ever have. I wanted to know how they decided what to do and how it adds meaning to their lives. Yet when I asked them about making a difference, I got some puzzled looks. These nine women, it seems, did not get caught up in grand notions of trying to make the world a better place. Generally, they just saw a need and stepped in to fill it.

Only when I asked the question this way did they push themselves to examine their motives and think, *What have I done to make a difference?* Several of them thanked me for asking the question.

THE QUESTION

What do you do to try to "make a difference"? Do you do volunteer work or give back to the community? If so, what is the importance of that to your life?

Isabelle

I've had many volunteer jobs, almost always with children. I think that's where it starts, with our children. They need a lot. Our culture is such that our kids just want more and more stuff. Somehow we've lost the innocence and adventure of childhood. Recently, I took my great-grandchildren to a neighborhood celebration where they had a lot of activities for kids, including those air bouncy things. I noticed a girl there, about fourteen, dressed in perfect shorts and shoes. She listened to her iPod the whole time, looking very bored.

I thought, *Is this where we are?* I know this is only one girl, but her attitude stands for what's happening to some kids. I just want to see children be themselves for as long as possible.

Back in the 1970s, I volunteered at a preschool started by a woman at my church. She was tutoring a black woman on how to read. The two of them started talking about children and reading, and they decided to start a preschool to help poor children prepare for school. I don't know how they did it. They got money and hired one person to be the first teacher, a wonderful, energetic woman. They started in a dinky little church in a poor central-city neighborhood.

My friend gathered a lot of women from our church and from her neighborhood and organized them to volunteer once a week and teach one class. There were four volunteers for every day, doing math, reading, social studies, and art—that meant twenty volunteers a week. In the beginning, we taught only four-year-olds. It was a prescribed method involving repetition, teaching numbers and letters. Every teacher did the same thing. The philosophy was that disadvantaged children already had lots of free time; what they needed was structure.

The next year, they got more funding and the program grew. They progressed through the years until they were paying the teachers and had several schools. I started as a volunteer and later got paid, though not a whole lot.

By then, the school was in a community center, and the other teachers teased me because I was the only white person. They marched me by a Black Panther house, teasing me by saying, "They're going to get you, Isabelle!" I was uncomfortable at first, until I got to know them. Those teachers liked to test me. They would hold teacher meetings at night, and I felt unsafe walking to my car. But nothing bad ever happened. And I made some good friends.

The program went on and eventually it even included kindergarten classes in the public schools—using the same structure and methods. It flourished for a long time. It was an amazing accomplishment for these two women, one of them illiterate. Eventually, the original volunteers dropped out and paid teachers took over.

I hope it made a difference—that the children learned something and that they had a good start by the time they got to school. At the very least, it helped their parents because they had somewhere to put their children while they were working. I don't think I had any marvelous fervor or idea about what I was doing. I did it because it was something I could do to help people. I just thought, *I like being around children. These little ones need taking care of, and here I am.*

Later, after we moved to Egypt, I would go with some other women out to Giza and wash babies. The mothers in poor neighborhoods would bring their babies to a clinic. Before the doctor examined the babies, we would wash and dress them. The clinic promised to give them a piece of baby clothing each time they came. The babies were swaddled, and we would unwrap them and lay them out. They would be kicking, and the moms would sit there laughing. We would also check their eyes for eye diseases. You can't imagine this clinic. It was grim and not especially clean, and there were benches full of people waiting for the doctor. It's a whole different world. I wanted to help somehow, and I enjoyed meeting these wonderful women.

When I lived in Los Angeles, I answered a rape crisis hotline. That was very disturbing. Often I was the first person they talked to. For the hotline, I was instructed to just listen and tell them where to go for help. I did it at home. I remember sitting on the floor and listening to these stories that to me were unbelievably awful. Sometimes I had to go with people to the hospital and the police station. I don't know that I was any help because I was always in shock about what was happening.

Joy

Do I make a difference? Yes, of course I try! I hope I do make a difference, but it is up to others to say so. It would be good to know if others appreciated my work.

I do truly enjoy working with people. I have heard others say that they hate committee work, and they avoid it. I may be strange because I truly like it. I have always volunteered and often have been given leadership duties, beginning in college on through to community, national and local church work.

I think committee work is very creative and can be wonderfully challenging, too. I enjoy getting the people in a group to pull together, and I like it when they feel like they are all, as a unit, getting credit for a job well done.

Anna

The motivation has been there from childhood because I grew up in the church and that was what was taught. We are given the gift of life: part of it is to live it and part of it is to share what we have with others who have less.

In addition, I was the oldest child who was supposed to take care of everybody else. So I had a dual motive. I was supposed to fix everybody's problems just because they were there. That's the not-so-healthy message I got. I still struggle with how to take care of myself and not just everybody else.

It is clear to me that we white Protestant people are the wealthy of the world, especially those of us who live in the U.S., and by golly because we follow Jesus we'd better share our time and money. There isn't a religion that doesn't teach some variation of "Do unto others as you would have them do unto you." Most of them add more definition to what that means: you are obliged to give and help those who have less.

I have not volunteered my time very much. I've either been raising children, going to seminary, or working as a chaplain. I worked on election boards for a number of years in the days before voting by mail. I did it because voting is a privilege we have in the U.S., and I wanted to help that happen.

I donate financially to several organizations, when I can. I help in the neighborhood when somebody's ill or in need. I give blood.

I have my name on the wall because I have given more than a hundred gallons. I'm pleased about it. I started back in 1967 when my son had major surgery. In recent years, I do it as frequently as I can.

Now that I'm retired, I think that I would like to be a volunteer in a particular area, but I can never decide which one. I will probably get involved helping women and children who have experienced domestic violence. And maybe help the homeless, too.

Oh, yes, and I knit—all the time. Everything I knit I give away. I knit for auctions, for all kinds of nonprofits. I knit for the homeless. Every night when we watch TV, I knit. I take my knitting in the car if we eat out. And if I'm going to a conference, it's the way I listen best. Knitting is a joy and now it's probably an addiction. The yarn is expensive, and I spend a good deal on it. I've got every size needle. The beads are not cheap. It adds up. It's a part of my financial commitment.

Eva

Oh my. If I could just bring a bit more joy into someone's life and eliminate even just a little bit of their pain or unpleasantness, I would feel like I contributed something.

Bringing peace into the world is perhaps one of the reasons why we are here. In any event, I'm trying not to cause more trouble, trying not to aggravate more people, and I hope to encourage more people to believe that it is possible to have a world without war— that it is definitely possible.

I just read a marvelous thing in a theosophical newsletter about the Jains in India. I don't know much about them, except that Jains try not to harm any living being. They even wear masks so they don't inadvertently breathe in a bug and end its life. The article said, "One can be a Hindu, a Muslim, a Christian and still in some way support and defend the idea of violence. One cannot be Jain and at the same time support and defend violence." Many who call themselves Christian do defend "just wars." I don't think war fits so well with Jesus's approach to life, but in a lot of Christian circles it's acceptable and encouraged. People are considered heroic if they do some of these things that I don't think are so wonderful.

According to this newsletter article, theosophists believe it is their duty "to gain wisdom, practice compassion, and be peaceful." I was so excited when I read that! I think this is why I am drawn to theosophy. The only thing theosophists have to accept is universal brotherhood and kinship. The very few theosophists that I know really do strive to gain wisdom and to be compassionate and peaceful. Those are my core values, too. I believe we can be deeply devoted to following Christ and, at the same time, appreciate the Holy Spirit, the same spirit that can be found in people of other faith or wisdom traditions. In today's world, I wonder if it may even be an imperative, if we are to be truly Christian.

Whether or not I'm making a difference, I don't know. But I'm hoping that by handing out flyers about nonviolence I am helping and not harming anything. We never know how effective we are. I believe that conversation is a powerful thing. If you share your heartfelt thoughts with someone, it makes a difference. When I hear about some of the people who are causing a lot of trouble, I keep hoping that if we send out good thoughts, somehow these thoughts might settle in on them.

That's why I was so unhappy about what we did to Osama bin Laden because now there is no chance that he could have an epiphany. If he had had a change of heart, what a difference that would have made! When you do an enemy in, you deny God a chance to work a miracle. There is a proverb that says, "Rejoice not when your enemy falls." Yet there was considerable rejoicing when bin Laden fell.

Gandhi said, "Prayer is not simply an old woman's idle amusement. Properly understood and applied, it is the most potent instrument of action." Some people don't pray to God, but they hold their very highest thoughts for the common good. That would be prayer, I think. Those higher thoughts might also be very potent instruments of action.

Those flyers we hand out—some of them I know end up in the

trash. But if just one gets through, it could do some good.

Some wise soul—I wonder who?—has noted that "We live not for ourselves but for the whole human race, and if we can help set that the tiniest notch higher on its upward course, it is enough." I hope that with Women in Black, by participating with other groups of people working toward improving our lot in life, and perhaps by disseminating Dudley Carter's exemplary life story, and having played a part in rearing two fine sons, I'm making a difference. Perhaps in some way it is helping to raise our collective consciousness—what some term our Christ-consciousness—even just a bit.

Susan

My husband and I both felt it was important to contribute to our community. You don't just live there and take. A medical practice is very demanding, and in the early days my husband was on duty most of the week and every other weekend. It fell in my bailiwick to be the person who contributed to the community, with both time and resources.

For us, responsibility was written across our foreheads and commitment was written across our chins. That was just a part of the way we grew up and the way we lived our lives. Giving back to community is a part of our value system. For example, I served on the county library board for eleven years. I worked for the PTA and was a den mother for six years. I put a ton of time into the church, serving at the local, regional, and national levels.

After I got my master's degree, I was asked to represent my denomination on the first ecumenical board of the theology school at a Catholic university. They had two boards, one that was Catholic and one that included ten or eleven denominations. That appealed to me because I believe in ecumenism. I believe that somehow, somewhere, some way, we who have belief in a supreme being must get together and understand each other. I did that for twelve or fourteen years. The school is now thriving, and it encourages people of different denominations to increase understanding and work together.

One person can't do it all. But it's better to light a candle than curse the darkness.

If you feel something needs to be done, put some time into it. Don't just sit and say, "I wish somebody would do something about this." That somebody might be you.

From what I know about life, you never know if what you're doing is going to make a difference. But you may find out, if you're lucky, years and years from now, or even six months from now. I had that happen to me once. I was attending a Bible class, and we had some interesting discussions. One day, I was sitting there and the woman next to me said, "I want you to know that what you said to me has almost saved my life." I have no idea what I said to her! You just never know.

Helping other people feeds my soul. When you give, you get a whole lot more than you give, over and over. If I can support somebody else, I want to do that. Recently, I've met many people who are dealing with spouses who have Alzheimer's disease, and they need support. How can you not reach out to people who are hurting? My husband says, "I don't know how people tell you the things they tell you." And I say, "More than anything, I really appreciate people, and I appreciate hearing what they have to say." I guess I'm a good listener.

Ruth

When I was on the Committee on Preparation for Ministry, I was an advocate for people considering ministry and going to seminary. I encouraged them to be who they were—not what they were supposed to be or expected to be. I think it was helpful to them. It was during the time when the church was torn by the controversy over the gay and lesbian issue, and I was able to be an encourager and advocate for people—particularly for one young woman who was lesbian. She now leads her own church. That was very gratifying to me.

When I was a younger woman, I did some tutoring in schools in the central city, and I also did some tutoring in the county jail. Those were not as comfortable for me as some of the other things I have done, but I was very glad I did them. I was pushing myself. I got great joy from being with the students and the prisoners. Also, I have been able to mentor some young people I know, helping them figure out who they were.

Any time that I do anything that I would consider halfway kind or compassionate, or giving or good, I consider that is part of my being a follower of Christ. Any good in me is because of that. I do believe that.

Katherine

When I went to Mount Holyoke, the president kept insisting that we were "uncommon women," that we were receiving an "uncommon education," and that he counted on us to go forth and do "uncommon things" for good in the world. I have friends who still feel burned by the phrase "uncommon women" because they feel they haven't done enough in the world to qualify. Some wouldn't think of coming back for a college reunion because they don't think they have anything "uncommon" enough to brag about, that they have made no real difference in the world to speak of.

The question of "What do you do to try to make a difference in the lives of others?" makes it sound as though you have an expectation, and I wonder how many women would perceive the question as a burden.

That said, I know how the admonition "to whom much is given, much shall be required" can resonate with those of us privileged enough to hear those words and realize they may be directed at us. It is only by the grace of God that I was born white, American, and straight. I've lived long enough to understand something of the other side of each of those privileges, and to be embarrassed by the way I assumed white, American, and straight were not only the easiest options, but kind of ordained as the best.

Falling in love with another woman was a huge challenge to all of these assumptions. Being with Marie has taught me the importance of being one's best self, no matter one's color, nationality, or orientation—and doing it with openness, pride, and humility. That is perhaps the greatest work I can do to make a difference in a world teetering on the brink of full acceptance of all persons.

I wrote my memoir, *The Last of the Good Girls: Shedding Convention, Coming Out Whole*, so that my grandchildren will have the story of how our family morphed from father/mother/two children into the much more complex—yet whole—family that it is. They get to have three grandmas on their mother's side! Now that I've released the book, I've been stunned to hear from readers, many of whom I don't even know, saying how much they appreciate my telling my story. My book seems to be making "a difference in the lives of others," and that thrills me.

MY TAKEAWAYS

Uncommon women—I'll say!

It surprised me to hear Katherine's reaction to my question—her response that it feels like a burden. That makes sense, yet none of the other women reacted that way.

To me, it seems admirable that these women responded with humility. None of them set out to brag; they had to think hard. And some of them, I happen to know, didn't mention half the things they had done. I had to push them to recall what they had done to help others—and when they did, the list was long and lively: washing babies in Egypt, creating a preschool in a poor urban area, helping set up an ecumenical seminary, writing a memoir that gives others courage, encouraging a lesbian to become a pastor, and writing and handing out flyers about nonviolence. They didn't take a "holier than thou" view that their lives had made more of a difference than most.

So many of the Christians I read about in the newspapers come off sounding narrow-minded and mean, attacking certain people and trying to restrict rights and behaviors. Yet my experience in getting to know these women—and others in the church—is just the opposite. They don't try to impose their views on others or save souls; they see a need and step in to fill it. From my years of experience as a journalist, I realize why that doesn't make the headlines. "Christian helps others" is not news. "Christian burns Korans" or "Christian shows up at military funerals mocking gays" is definitely news—but also gives a warped view of Christianity to anyone outside the church. It puts out the idea that all Christians are hypocrites.

I found nothing hypocritical in these nine women. If anything, they wondered if their volunteer work had made a difference. The babies they washed in Egypt and the poor preschoolers have grown up now, and they probably have no idea how these women helped them. But it's still worthwhile to go out into the world and do good.

Chapter 20

Seeking Peace and Hope

PHEW. AFTER ANGER, dark places, and failure, it's nice to focus on something positive, like peace and hope—and inspiration.

In the midst of stressful lives, when we're always running behind schedule and have fifty million things on our to-do list, it's good to think about ways to bring our hearts to a place of peace. And when bad news splashes across the newspapers, television, and our computer screens, how can we restore our sense of hope?

THE QUESTION

When are you most at peace? What keeps you moving forward into hope? Where do you look for inspiration?

Ruth

I am most at peace, I think, with a book or a pen in my hand. When I am out of doors, either gardening or sitting in my old blue chair, listening to the chickadees. When I have cooked up a stew and am sitting around the table with my family. When I am talking with a friend, with someone I love and trust. Being with people that I love helps bring my heart back to peace.

I look for inspiration in the ordinary: in the ordinary beauty of the day, in the details of family relationships, in nature and my garden. Think of some of the poets, like Mary Oliver, and how beautifully they capture the ordinary. That's what I love to write about. I like to dwell in the beauty of the ordinary.

Eva

One thing that has really helped me is a benediction recited at the end of Anglican services I attended as a youth. I remember it as this: "Go out into the world in peace. Have courage. Hold on to what is good. Return no one evil for evil. Strengthen the fainthearted. Support the weak. Help the suffering. Honor all people. Love and serve the Lord, rejoicing in the power of the Holy Spirit."

Very often in my later life, I've felt so low that I've been reluctant to even leave the house. Then that benediction would come to me, urging me to "Go!" Not just go, but "Go out in peace!" And "Have courage!" That blessing has given me courage very, very often.

Seeking peace and growing in hope has become a big thing in my life. Years ago, I was fortunate to become a close, personal friend of Santa Claus—also known as Bertil Valley. Bertil was a loyal patron of the artist Dudley Carter. At a time when Dudley was homeless, Bertil and his wife gave Dudley a place to stay. Then Bertil circulated a petition and moved our county to name Dudley Carter their first artist-in-residence, assuring him of a place to live and work for the rest of his life.

Bertil truly was Santa Claus. His hair and his beard were white, long, and flowing. His eyes were sparkly blue. And he was full of "ho, ho, hos." In the Christmas season, Bertil donned his plush red and white suit, plumped himself up with pillows, and played Santa for the Seattle Seahawks and the American Heart Association. But no matter what the season, he went about quietly doing good wherever he saw a need. When a friend's young daughter was in the hospital being treated for cancer, Bertil put on his Santa suit and brought joy to her and her fellow patients, even though it was July. If anyone ever tries to tell me that there is no Santa Claus,

I'll argue, "Oh yes there is. I know Santa Claus personally!" Santa Claus exists in everyone who has a deep desire to make life better.

One time I asked Bertil how he managed to do so much good in this world. He responded, "Ah, it's not all that much. It's not world peace." Something in the way he said that, something in the way he looked at me, made me think that I need to see what I can do for world peace.

After 9/11, having met Jihad, I became concerned about peoples' attitudes toward Muslims. It seemed to me that the media's take on Islam was instilling undue fear in Americans. And, without giving it enough thought, our nation went to war in Afghanistan. When it appeared that we were going to send troops into Iraq, I couldn't stand it. President Bush's "shock-and-awe" plan really shocked me. I had to do something. I wrote a letter to the President, imploring him not to attack Iraq. I got back a "Thanks for your support" letter—so discouraging. I figured that approach was useless.

But along came another outlet. Our church newsletter carried a notice about a silent vigil for peace and justice. A group of women, part of an international network known as Women in Black that began in Israel in 1988, was standing on a street corner downtown, quietly mourning victims of all war and violence and promoting peace and justice. I thought that that was something I could do. Perhaps it would be more effective than we realized. So for over ten years, I've stood with that dedicated group of kindred spirits who appear at noon every Saturday on the same corner, our city's busiest intersection, offering passersby flyers bearing timely articles, quotations, and arguments in favor of peace. More often than not, passersby express their thanks and encouragement. There's reason to be hopeful.

Could it be possible that when we take our best thoughts and our hopes out into the world, our collective consciousness is raised and we connect to what Harvard author Steven Pinker calls "the better angels of our nature"? Some physicists now say that thoughts have power; there is energy in thought. Will all that good energy have the power to bring about world peace? I believe it can. I believe it will—eventually!

When it comes to seeking peace and remaining hopeful, I'm going to try to avoid the pessi-mystics and seek the company of all the opti-mystics I can find.

Susan

I feel very grounded most of the time—if that's what you call at peace.

I'm grounded, but the peace definitely has a wavy surface. Anything can change in the blink of an eye, you know. Last night, I was watching little gymnasts on TV. One girl was doing her vaults, and she's done this maybe three thousand times perfectly, and then she fell. I am at peace right now, but maybe the phone will ring and one of the kids will be in dire straits. Things go wrong, and to me the most important thing is that you've got to accept yourself and accept the situation in which you find yourself.

I think being grounded is much more important than being at peace.

Isabelle

Sam and I used to go to the jazz festival in Sun Valley every year. We'd listen to music all day for four days, from ten in the morning to ten at night. I always admired those musicians. That's an inspiration to me—that and the symphony. Sam used to go with me. Now I go by myself.

I find music can be very helpful to pain. I don't play any; I play the piano but only for myself, and I can't sing. I always admire people who are musical: to have that music inside of you and to be able to bring it out in people. That's an inspiration in me—to hear really good music or see really good theater. I love to go and see somebody who captures the spirit of another person. That to me is inspirational and can make me feel really happy inside.

Or just go look for birds. Birds are always a solace for me because it's quiet and you find the unexpected. I love the feeling of amazement when I find an unexpected bird—or when I watch any bird, doing what birds do. I still do that sometimes. I go to the nearby park and see what little one I can find poking in the bushes. I think those two things are my solace.

And little kids—I find little children so free! They have just a wonderful way of expressing themselves. Or they're shy and you see them come out. I have these drawings on the refrigerator from my grandson. I like to see how children start drawing and how their drawings progress. I feel good when I'm around little ones. Sometimes I get tired, but on the whole it's fun to be around children.

Jane

I feel most at peace when I lie down to sleep. I also feel a lot of peace when I work outside in the garden and in the yard; I like that particularly.

I tend to be hopeful. I can think of times I've been disappointed and have had to face hard realities: *Well, you are going to have to live with that. Yes, this person is not going to get better*, I have told myself. One long-time friend of mine has dementia, and I've had to accept that I won't have a relationship with her anymore because she will never again recognize me. But I still hope.

I find myself being hopeful when I'm around young people, with their energy. It's great.

Anna

I would love to get to hold a baby every day. That would just thrill my soul. I just have an itch for them. Watch what women do: when a newborn is in the room, the women just flock. There's this "I've got to hold them" thing. It never goes away. It is such a delight to watch. Babies are content with whatever we're doing, bouncing along or playing. Because they're so dependent, there is no resistance on their part. If they're bouncing along on the hip, so what. If they're having to sit and wait in a stroller, they'll let you know if that's too long. Watching that is truly a pleasure.

Joy

What brings me to a place of peace? Lots of things, but for me, the major thing that destroys peace is the TV. It is intrusive and full of either negative news images or stupid, inane stuff. So I have discontinued my cable service. I know that it is totally radical—too much for most people—but I have not missed it for nearly a year now. I keep up with the news by reading it. I began to think about this when wondering why I was so supremely happy at my summer house. I realized it is a place of renewal because I am closer to God's creation while there, watching the lake at sunrise and sunset, pacing along the paths I've made for Zen walking, reading in the swing, walking round the lake. I feel at peace, oh yes, especially when sharing these quiet times with friends.

Writing also brings me peace and hope. First of all, it gets out the negative: anger, grief, tension, problems. When I go inside myself and let words bleed out of my fingertips, then I can discover what may have been hidden from me. I am often surprised by what comes out. For this, I seek quiet time. Living alone provides this advantage: more opportunity for uninterrupted time.

It's very important to learn to be in the moment. We live by the clock so much and by the calendar and by our schedules and our future. Too often we don't take the day, the hour, even twenty minutes to be in the present. For me, time in the car sometimes can do that, if I don't turn on the radio.

Sometimes I have composed haiku poems while driving. I wrote a series while driving across Spain and encouraged my car mates to do it too. I thought, *This place is just priceless. Every part of this trip has a message, and I want to capture it*. Haikus are only seventeen syllables or less, so I can remember them and write the words down later. This is a great mental exercise: think about this particular point of the trip, what's here, be open to why it is resonating. It's as good as or better than taking a photograph!

Also, I belong to wonderful groups, most of them church friends. I belong to a meditation group, and it is very powerful to sit in a room with others, deep in silence. I'm reading more and more about how people live longer when they meditate. We are healthier. Scientists are analyzing brain waves to see what meditation does. I'm just lucky that I managed to live in a place where friends were doing this and they said, "Come along," and I did.

Photography is another great way to focus on hope and peace. When you get rid of all the extraneous stuff around your chosen subject, you can pick up colors or perhaps the detail of a line that you didn't see. God made such an enormously beautiful creation, and we sometimes just walk through it without seeing it and feeling thankful.

Katherine

Peace has a lot to do with contentment. These days, I'm at peace a lot of the time, with Marie. We share an incredible intimacy and spaciousness. Our relationship is like our house. There's room for both of us, and that's very peaceful.

I'm at peace having coffee in the morning on my patio. The older I get, the more solitude means to me. This is from somebody who lived most of her life thinking she was an extrovert. It's come as a surprise. I've always loved being in nature, and now I think that's part of it, too. I don't need to be in a lot of meetings or with a whole bunch of people. I'm not lonely when I'm alone. My friend Tom the Irishman used to say, "I just spent the day musing." That's peaceful for me: musing time.

I think that the older we get, the more introverted we get. It has something to do with peace and solitude. If I don't have enough solitude, I get jangly and jumpy.

What's a source of my hope? I'd say faith. I don't know all the answers, but I trust that there is a source that does have the answers, and in whose hands I ultimately am held.

Also grandchildren, the coming generations, are a source of hope. I'm terribly impressed with these young kids, with their sense of environmental stewardship. I wish I could believe that they could bring about world peace.

Young people and faith and friends—I can't not go back to friends. Having a group of people you can laugh with is important. Our group of chosen sisters gets together every month on the third Monday, whether we need to or not. It used to be brunch and now we start about eleven, so it's more like lunch. If we part by six, that's an early day. We never run out of things to talk about or laugh about. There is nothing as hopeful as having friends you can share and laugh with.

I can't say enough, for all of you who are in your forties or fifties or whatever, to just find yourself and cultivate and nurture certain friends. It's lifesaving.

MY TAKEAWAYS

Aaah. To me, these selections are like a soft breeze.

It's interesting how many of these women find peace in solitude: "musing time," meditation, being in the moment, noticing nature, writing haikus, and photographing God's creation. They also find peace in quiet activities like gardening, sleep, and exercise.

But others find peace—and hope—by spending time with loved ones and chatting with close friends, supportive groups, grandchildren, and young people.

Susan reminds us that peace has a "wavy surface." Anything can change in the blink of an eye. For her, the goal is not to be at peace. She aims to be grounded, so she can handle such disruptions with a steady mind.

Then there's Santa Claus: a powerful example of a person who gives of himself to make life better for others for nothing in return. Of course, it's not world peace.

For that, there's the Women in Black, standing on street corners in cities around the world, holding signs, in a quiet vigil against all war. Standing on a street corner with a sign doesn't bring about world peace. But perhaps there is energy in thought—and in letting others know our thoughts about peace.

When you're hungry for inspiration, try seeking out some of these:

+ Listen to music you enjoy, whether jazz, the symphony, opera, or something completely different.

+ Enjoy nature: especially trees and birds.

+ Revel in the beauty of the ordinary, as observed and captured by poets.

+ Talk and laugh with friends who encourage you.

+ Spend time with little kids, with their delightful way of expressing themselves.

+ Hold a baby.

FINAL THOUGHTS

AFTER NINE INTERVIEWS over warm cups of tea with women I admire, my head was spinning. It took me many months to sift through their comments and make sense of them. Now that I've finished, I sit back and ponder: What did I learn? Am I any wiser than I was before I began these interviews?

What resonates most clearly for me is the importance of asking. I found that when I made an intentional effort to pursue wisdom, when I asked deep questions that matter to me, I gained fresh insights into everyday living and found mental tools I can use next time I feel angry or sad or face a tough situation.

I was both warmed and surprised by the variety of responses from these women, each so different from the others. Yet they all have reached their seventies or eighties as thoughtful, resilient people who have, by and large, figured out how to maintain good relationships with those they love. They've dealt with tough times—mostly far tougher than anything I've faced—and they've learned from them. With humility, honesty, and humor, they continue to ask questions and search for better answers.

Among older women, I found, there is an untapped well of people too wise to try to force their wisdom on others. Many women of this generation, trained in the 1950s to be helpmates to their husbands, have lived their lives under the radar. If everyone was getting along at home, they didn't feel the need to seek achievement in the larger world. But when they did venture out, with modest expectations, they were surprised and delighted with what they could do. In that sense, they can be a wonderful source of comfort and inspiration to younger women.

The very process of interviewing these women has enriched my life. They make the future look appealing and inviting—and promise the possibility of contentment at the end.

Every person who reads these pages comes from a different set of life experiences. What seems wise and relevant to one reader may seem obvious or off base to another. I hope that the variety of personalities I interviewed will mean that every reader can relate to at least one.

The best way to seek wisdom, I'm convinced, is to find your own group of wise people and spend time with each one, asking questions. Look around your community and locate the wise people in your life, men or women whose lives you admire. Perhaps for you that means calm and unstressed. Perhaps it means adventurous and unafraid. When we choose people we perceive as wise, that says a lot about what kind of lives we aspire to.

Ask them to open their lives to you, to tell you what they've learned that might be useful to you. Feel free to use my questions or make up your own. Visit with your mother, your aunt, any older woman or man whose life reflects some measure of grace in your eyes. And consider sharing what you have learned from them—at the very least with your own circle of friends.

I found that when I put myself in a listening mode, when I stopped trying to insert my own opinions, I opened my ears to what these women had to say—whether I agreed with it or not. I didn't argue back or bring up my own life experiences. I just listened.

Sometimes I felt intimidated about asking for these interviews. I knew all of these women, but I really didn't know much about their lives. I had to build up my courage to ask if they'd be willing to sit for a few hours and answer intimate, personal questions—and let me share those answers with the world. I expected at least some to say no. No one did. In fact, some of them opened up far more than I expected and entrusted me with wrenching stories and deep secrets. I planned to interview a lot more women—and I had many more that I intended to ask—but I was afraid of being overwhelmed.

Along the way, I realized that reaching for the wisdom of elders is worthwhile and satisfying. Whoever you are, and whatever wisdom you are seeking, you will find wisdom in those around you, if you dare to ask.

So here is my challenge to you, the reader: Go forth and seek wisdom. Start your own "wisdom project." If you dare to ask, the results may surprise, delight, and enrich you.

Like luminaria along a pathway, your chosen elders may help you to see more clearly the road ahead.

BOOK CLUB

DISCUSSION QUESTIONS

1. Do you think all people get wiser as they get older? Why or why not?

2. When you think of people you know who seem "unwise," what is it about their behavior that makes them seem that way? What would it take for them to change?

3. Think of some wise people in your life, a generation older than you. Have you ever sat down and asked them questions like this? What would happen if you did?

4. Which of these twenty questions speaks most to you at this stage of your life? How did you react to the responses given by the nine women to this key question?

5. Which of these nine women did you relate to the most? The least? Why?

6. In the introduction, the author attempts to define wisdom. How would you define it differently?

7. What's your view on happiness? Is it an inborn trait, a response to circumstances, or a choice?

8. All these women are involved with their church. To what extent is their advice relevant to people who are not Christian or who are not involved with organized religion?

9. These women had widely varying responses to the question about raising teenagers, yet similar responses to that about relating to adult children. Why do you think that is?

10. Most of these women said the best way to deal with adult children is to refrain from giving advice unless asked. Yet some adult children need or want advice. Under what circumstances should parents give advice to their adult children?

11. Almost all these women made major life changes at midlife. Do you think this is harder or easier for women to do than men? Why?

12. Which advice or story struck you as particularly useful or memorable?

ACKNOWLEDGMENTS

ON THE COVER of this book, I insisted on the words "gathered by" because the wisdom in this book is not my own. It bubbled up from the nine women I interviewed, and I extend heartfelt thanks to all nine of them for their willingness to sit down with me and answer a battery of tough, probing, intimate questions. I was delighted by their candor and awed by their generosity in agreeing to share their personal stories and tough dilemmas with me and with the world. I appreciate their time, their support, and their willingness to review and refine their own comments. In a sense, they are the coauthors of this book. Thank you to all nine of them, who humored me by accepting pseudonyms for this book. I wanted them to feel safe opening up their hearts and sharing their losses, regrets, joys, and hopes. And thanks to the many other wise women I know, whose wisdom would also have enriched this book—if only I had had the courage to ask them.

During the five years since I began this book, I fell off track a few times, and I deeply appreciate those who encouraged me and helped me to get moving again: Katy Ehrlich, Susan Little, Cris Wilkinson, and Mary Ann Woodruff. Their warm suggestions and editorial comments were invaluable, as were those of the Reverend Janet DeWater. I appreciate the transcription work of Kelly Wilkinson and Carly Wilkinson, and the excellent professional editing of Meredith Bailey. What makes this book pop off the shelves is the gorgeous cover design by the creative genius of Kathy Campbell.

Since my childhood, Lynn Joachim Bell and her mother, Louise Kyle Joachim, have shown me wisdom in action. I'm grateful for this lifelong friendship and to Lynn for showing me the way.

Finally, I thank my friends in Hope Circle, who sustained me with their enthusiasm, helped me formulate these questions, and expressed eagerness to hear the answers from these women, whom they also admire as wise.

I'd like to dedicate this book to the memory of my mother, Marny Jones, and to the women of her generation who raised us and inspired us.

And to you, dear readers, please keep in touch through my Wisdom column at *www.dorijonesyang.com.* I'd love to hear the stories and insights you discover in your own wisdom project.

—Dori Jones Yang

BOOKS YOU MIGHT ENJOY

Listed below are some books on wisdom that inspired me. I think you'll enjoy them, too.

Borg, Marcus J. *The Heart of Christianity: Rediscovering a Life of Faith.*

Carson, Rick. *Taming Your Gremlin: A Surprisingly Simple Method for Getting Out of Your Own Way.*

Chittister, Joan. *The Gift of Years: Growing Older Gracefully.*

Duerk, Judith. *Circle of Stones: Woman's Journey to Herself.*

Gruenewald, Mary Matsuda. *Becoming Mama-San: 80 Years of Wisdom.*

Kushner, Harold. *Who Needs God* and *When Bad Things Happen to Good People.*

Remen, Rachel Naomi. *My Grandfather's Blessings: Stories of Strength, Refuge, and Belonging.*

Richmond, Lewis. *Aging as a Spiritual Practice: A Contemplative Guide to Growing Older and Wiser.*

Schachter-Shalomi, Zalman, and Ronald Miller. *From Ageing to Sage-ing: A Profound New Vision of Growing Older.*

Seligman, Martin. *Authentic Happiness: Using the New Positive Psychology to Realize Your Potential for Lasting Fulfillment.*

The Arbinger Institute. *The Anatomy of Peace: Resolving the Heart of Conflict.*

Valliant, George E. *Aging Well: Surprising Guideposts to a Happier Life from the Landmark Harvard Study of Adult Development.*

Woodruff, Mary Ann. *The Last of the Good Girls: Shedding Convention, Coming Out Whole.*

ABOUT THE AUTHOR

DORI JONES YANG drew on twenty years of experience as a reporter to conduct interviews with these nine women. She began her journalism career with her hometown newspaper, the *Youngstown Vindicator*, and worked on *The Daily Princetonian* during college. During two years in Singapore, she taught English, studied Mandarin Chinese, and traveled around Asia. After earning a master's degree in international relations, she joined *Business Week*, which sent her to Hong Kong to cover the opening of China to the outside world. After fifteen years with *Business Week*, she later covered technology for *U.S. News & World Report*.

Although raised in a church in Ohio, she was "unchurched" for twenty years. After moving to the Seattle area in 1990, she joined a church and became active in it, chairing the adult education committee and learning about faith as an adult. She has written five books, including a business book about Starbucks Coffee, a children's book about a Chinese immigrant girl, two historical novels set in China at the time of Marco Polo, and a book of oral histories of Chinese Americans. She and her husband have a grown daughter, as well as two adult children from his first marriage.

For more information, see *www.dorijonesyang.com*.